HOW MY NEIGHBOR WORSHIPS

Also by Gail Reitenbach

Blown Away: A First Year in Santa Fe

HOW MY NEIGHBOR WORSHIPS

A GRAND TOUR OF FAITH COMMUNITIES

Gail Reitenbach

Right Hand Communications
Santa Fe, New Mexico

Published by Right Hand Communications LLC, Santa Fe, New
Mexico
www.righthandcom.com

Printed in the United States of America

Design and cover images by Gail Reitenbach

Library of Congress Control Number: 2006929528

Cataloging information:
Reitenbach, Gail.
How my neighbor worships: a grand tour of faith communities / Gail
Reitenbach
1. Religions. 2. Spirituality.   3. Worship. I. Title.

ISBN-10
0-9786842-0-6
ISBN-13
978-0-9786842-0-4

CONTENTS

For all who have a curiosity about religious faiths and traditions. For all who have wanted to make a similar journey. For all who live where they can't easily make such a journey. For all who are fearful about what they might discover on such a journey. For all who are certain that such journeys are wrong (or worse). For all who believe and all who disbelieve. For all serious-minded folks. For all who want a lighter look at the subject of religion. For all good reasons. For friends like Sharon Gillespie and Jody Berman, who encouraged me and shared my curiosity. And especially for my spirit mate, David Prochnow, who shares my interest in spirituality, faith, and religion—and who understands that those terms are not necessarily synonymous.

Prologue: Church-hopper

Church-hopping: Compare with barhopping.

✦ ✦ ✦

The goal of barhopping isn't particularly lofty. It's merely to add variety to an evening by sampling the libations and atmosphere of multiple bars. I had no grand goals when I started church-hopping either. As a newcomer to Santa Fe, and as someone who had had church responsibilities for years, I suddenly found myself without any particular demands on my Sunday mornings.

My husband, David, and I had agreed to take a break from church for a while. We had moved from Boulder, Colorado, in the fall of 2003 so David could start a new career in New Mexico. We had been part-time church musicians for the fifteen years we had lived in Boulder—he as a Lutheran choir director and I as the organist at the same church and, before that, as a substitute organist in several other churches of various denominations. For fifteen years we worked our regular weekday jobs, planned for and led choir rehearsal on Wednesday evenings, and then led Sunday morning worship. People who aren't musicians, especially those who aren't paid to be on time as musicians, don't always understand that, much as we might enjoy music, a music job is work—a four-letter word. Adding a church job to a Monday-to-Friday job means working six days a week. Even on the seventh day, instead of resting, I often had to practice. The point is, after fifteen years, we needed a sabbatical.

I also needed a new way to relate to worship. I had started playing for Sunday School services when I was nine. At age twelve, I began playing part-time for church services. Throughout high school and college, I was a substitute or part-time organist. When I wasn't playing, I was often singing in a choir. In the first couple of months after leaving our Boulder music posts, when we did attend a service, it felt odd to sit in the pews. Worship was almost a disembodied experience because we weren't involved in making it happen. We couldn't help but critique the organists and choir directors, sometimes fighting the urge to hip-check them out of their space and take over. Gradually, we quelled that impulse, but I, at least, felt a bit worthless just sitting in the pew and following along with the rest of the sheep.

Maybe that's why I hit upon a new way to make work out of worship.

After I'd decided to go church-hopping, it was easy to come up with a raft of justifications.

One of my strongest incentives for undertaking this tour was to test the oft-repeated claim that Santa Fe is a spiritual place. Yes, the landscape can be awesome, conducive to reflection and meditation (at least if you're a visitor who doesn't have to worry about making a living here). And yes, a dozen pueblo Indian communities have practiced their sacred rites nearby for centuries. But I've always been skeptical of claims that one locale is somehow more sacred than another. Surely Mother Teresa would have argued that point. Might it be that Santa Fe's much-vaunted spirituality is as much a construct as the quaint pueblo architectural style imposed upon the town by city leaders early in the twentieth century for the sake of creating a tourist lure?

My mother-in-law also provided an impetus for this exercise when she visited for Christmas 2003. During the course of a conversation whose context I've forgotten, she pronounced, "This is a Christian nation!" I promptly retorted, "No, it's not; it's a free nation in which the separation of church and state is guaranteed, and that's a very good thing!"

The exchange raised an unspoken question for me: How could I love my neighbor as myself if I didn't know anything about how my neighbor worshipped?

In the midst of that same discussion, I said, "For most people, their religion is an accident of birth." What I meant was that most people practice the religion that their parents adhere to—their birth religion is more likely than not to become the religious path they follow throughout their lives, if they follow such a path at all. But in North America, at least, the religion one is born into doesn't have to be one's religious destiny.

Another reason for exploring non-Lutheran faith traditions was to see if and when worship addressed one of the main motives for any kind of religious practice: to feel some connection with the spiritual realm—to experience joy, the divine. How often do worshippers truly find that in a worship service? I wondered. For me, music had often been the conduit for intimations of the divine.

I found it relevant that the idea for this book arrived at the beginning of Lent. In some Christian traditions it's customary to give up something for Lent. Chocolate and smoking are perennial favorites. However, a few years ago, Mark Peterson, the pastor at the church we served in Boulder, suggested in a Lenten sermon that we "take something on" for Lent. He probably had in mind some sort of service project or spiritual discipline. Though I looked at my grand tour of Santa Fe faith communities more as a research project than a spiritual discipline or spiritual seeking, it would be a type of Lenten discipline.

Finally, if I were going to spend the rest of my life as a Lutheran, I wanted to know what I was missing. Before David and I ended up working at the same church, I had served as a substitute organist, on average, every third Sunday. When I wasn't working, I sang in David's choir. Whenever choir or congregation members would gripe about their church, I'd say that everyone should visit a different church in town at least twice a year and that, if they did so, they would realize just how good they had it—that no church is perfect. So, if I were going to claim that my birth faith is the right faith for me, I needed some basis for saying so.

Why not just read books about different denominations and religions? I could have, but books about religion are about as far removed from the reality of religious practice as books about sex are from sex. The experience of each depends a great deal on the people involved. I wanted to see how faith traditions are enacted in real life, not how they're written about.

For most of us, I suspect, no two Lutheran congregations—or Baptist or Religious Science congregations—would appeal to us in exactly the same way. Despite sharing a brand name, there's always a human factor at work. The individuals and congregations shaping the large and small details of how worship is expressed account for obvious and subtle differences between assemblies gathering under the same name. It would be unfair, then, to make assumptions about entire religious traditions based upon what I experienced in one place on one day.

Similarly, this book recounts my experiences in and responses to particular faith communities under specific conditions; had you visited each service the same day I did—even if you, too, were raised Lutheran—your reactions may have been different. I'm not suggesting that my assessments of what I saw and heard are "correct." Rather, I acknowledge that our religious and spiritual beliefs cannot help but frame the way we perceive new worship events. I also believe that first-hand experience with unfamiliar worship traditions can be useful in helping us refine—or sometimes redefine—our understandings of our own and others' beliefs.

Although I've been thoroughly immersed in Lutheranism since birth, I've never been one to accept any belief unquestioningly, and

I've never been wholeheartedly doctrinaire. As a graduate student I could never become a disciple of any particular literary theory—even feminist theory—because each brand seemed to supply a key to some but not all of a literary work's treasures. As a result, each chapter of my dissertation borrowed the insights of a different analytical methodology. Neither have I taken Christian dogma at face value. In college, Professor William Narum, who taught a philosophy of religion class, acknowledged that the unexamined faith is not worth having. I don't remember anything else I learned in his class, but I do remember his affirmation of a truth that I'd long held quietly.

As you may have gathered by now, my tone throughout this book, which describes and reflects upon my experiences of church-hopping in Santa Fe, is alternately (and sometimes simultaneously) reverent and irreverent. I try not to criticize gratuitously anything I saw or experienced, yet because religious communities are composed of human beings, the profane does infiltrate the sacred. If you disagree with anything you encounter on these pages, know that I intend no disrespect to any faith community. Rather than being a critique of various faith traditions, this book presents an experiment in first-hand comparative religion whose goal was to see what I would learn from the journey about myself and others.

I often chose the largest church in a given denomination—in hopes that it would have the best music program—or the closest, to see which churches were convenient, should I decide that I liked another path better than Lutheranism. To impose some degree of evenhandedness on my observations, I planned to focus on specific elements of each worship service. What kind of greeting would I receive? Would it be friendly but not probing? Would I be allowed anonymity but be made to feel welcome? What age were the congregants? Was the median age skewed toward retirees or families with young children, or was there a mix of generations? What about wine and women? Were women visible participants and officiants? Was a meal shared, and if so, with what bread and wine? (White and rosé wines always seem to imply that Jesus was anemic the day he gave his blood.)

Then there were the three Ms: message, music, and money. These are, after all, the core of most worship experiences. The message and music are the most evident aspects of a religious brand, and as a musician, I had an inherent bias toward the importance of music in worship.

I studiously avoided researching each religious group, because I didn't want this to become an academic exercise. The degree of background research I conducted after a visit was no more than the average church explorer might do and was mostly limited to checking a group's Web site. This almost anti-scholarly attitude may seem perverse considering that I'm an English Ph.D. who once tangled with excruciatingly abstruse literary theory. But anyone who's honest with herself will admit that the choice of a place of worship is made on the basis of feeling as much as thinking. Of course, knowing a religious body's history and traditions can deepen one's understanding and appreciation of it, but ultimately, those seeking a spiritual home (rather than just a social center or networking group) choose a congregation because of how it makes them *feel.*

In one respect this enterprise did seem like academic work. I've never had a powerful memory for verbatim speech, and I often have difficulty remembering people's names. Undertaking this task required me to replay specific phrases in my mind to fix them there for transcription after a service ended. I had never paid such close attention to sermons in my life as I did from March to October 2004.

St. Bede's Episcopal Church, March 7, 2004

I began my grand tour of faith communities with an Episcopal church, because Lutherans and Episcopalians have a "full communion" relationship, which means that not only can members of one church receive communion in the other, but their clergy are recognized in each others' pulpits.

In the interest of full disclosure, I'd already been to an Episcopal church in Santa Fe before I began this project. Two months after David and I moved to Santa Fe, we had attended a Christmas carol service at the downtown Church of the Holy Faith. We knew it was the final Sunday that composer and music director Gerald Near and organist Michael Case were presiding over the music, so we thought the service would be a grand finale. Unfortunately, it fizzled like wet fireworks. The choir sang one Near composition that was unmemorable and lacking in Advent or Christmas spirit. (The organ selection by Near was more engaging.) The rest of the choral selections were from tired old Anglican repertoire that barely nodded to the twentieth century let alone the twenty-first. Though the organ was adequate for the space, Case barely changed registrations for the hymns, never mind providing variation or ornamentation for hymn verses. I had expected more from these "luminaries," as the local paper's music critic had dubbed them.

What's more, the rector's sermon was narcolepsy-inducing, and there's just no excuse for dullness in the Advent and Christmas season. The tension in the air as the rector bade public farewell to the two musicians told me that Near and Case would probably make finer music in Arizona, where they were moving.

In light of an underwhelming experience at the purported flagship Episcopal church, I didn't have high hopes for St. Bede's.

✦ ✦ ✦

Though it's not uncommon to have an unpaved parking lot in Santa Fe, I was new enough to town that it still struck me as rather rustic to be parking amid chamisa and juniper shrubs on what would surely be gummy muck if we ever got rain again.

Inside St. Bede's, the window-framed octagonal sanctuary was decorated for Lent with purple paraments. Elk antlers sat on the altar, draped in purple. Someone completely unfamiliar with liturgical churches and the symbolism of Lent might think the antlers were more than a bit odd—a sign, perhaps, of some pagan ritual or a nod to "Santa Fe style"—like the sun-bleached cow skulls that sometimes hang over local fireplaces. I suspect that the antlers were intended to symbolize the casting off of our old life of sin. Other Lenten symbols drawn from nature often include bare branches and denuded trees. Even though they're intended as visual metaphors, I've always liked the way such natural elements can't help being what they are—elements of nature, signs of our bonds with the natural world, and tacit recognition that one of the most profound ways we can come to know the creative power of God is through the grandeur and mystery of creation.

I went to the second service of the day, thinking the odds were higher that the choir would sing at the later service, and I was right. The choir, however, was a very modest assembly: one man, who was joined by the choir director/organist on the bass clef lines, and a handful of women. Their long and tedious introit was from the hymnal, which hasn't changed in decades. Together with the *Book of Common Prayer,* the service books can't help but give worship a dated tone. The hymn choices, however, were sound, given the options available, and my favorite was the gradual hymn, "O Day of Peace

That Dimly Shines," sung to the tune "Jerusalem," which always makes me think of the movie *Monty Python and the Holy Grail* and seems so quintessentially Anglican.

I hadn't expected the sermon to be personally meaningful. It was, after all, just another Sunday service. But the Reverend Madelynn Kirkpatrick surprised me. She spoke without a microphone, without notes, and without a pulpit; in fact, the sanctuary had only a lectern for the lesson. The absence of a pulpit created a closer physical relationship between the preacher and worshippers.

Kirkpatrick, the associate rector, took the kernel of her sermon from a line in the day's first reading from Genesis, in which "a deep sleep fell upon Abram, and a deep and terrifying darkness descended upon him." In the course of her homily, she tied that experience of a "deep and terrifying darkness" to Christ's experience and to the promise that God's love would always penetrate that darkness. She also referred to the gospel lesson from Luke and began by noting the "confused origins" of some of Christ's words in that lesson. For those unfamiliar with how the books of the Bible came to be the books of the Bible, such commentary is important to acknowledge that these texts were constructed by humans well after the events they describe.

The part of her sermon that hit me right between the eyes, though, was when she spoke about choices and about a time when it's too late for choices. She talked about people who say, "I always wanted to write a book," or "I always meant to tell that person I loved him." In such serendipity I can't help but see the Spirit. Here was this person I'd never met reminding me, on the first day of my research for this project, that I didn't want to be one of those people who had such regrets.

The manner in which St. Bede's celebrated the Eucharist was familiar in its texts if not its music. I joined the others at the communion rail and received the old-fashioned wafer and red wine.

Though the four acolytes were junior high girls, and a few children joined the service after the sermon, the worshippers were mostly of late middle age and older. The most striking thing about the service was that all the officiants—presiding minister, deacon, and acolytes—were female.

At the close of the service, Kirkpatrick began her benediction with the words, "God the Mother and Father of us all. . . ." Decades ago, I heard female Lutheran pastors pronounce such a benediction, but it's been far too long since I've heard God described that way in any church.

There was lots of visiting in the sanctuary after worship. Obviously, the note at the top of the bulletin to "Please enter and leave the sanctuary quietly" was being soundly ignored. I was greeted warmly by both staff persons in the postservice receiving line.

After the postlude ended I stopped to tell the organist, Fritz Anders, that I'd enjoyed his playing. Even though the church has an electronic instrument rather than a pipe organ, Anders used it to its fullest and played musically. He had selected a difficult Marcel Dupre prelude, created interludes before the final stanzas of hymns, chose energized but singable tempos, and offered a rousing postlude on the Lenten hymn "In the Cross of Christ I Glory."

St. Bede's taught me that the criteria I had planned to use in studying this and other churches might be less informative than the unplanned elements of my church-hopping experiences.

The church's mission statement proclaims in part, "We accept and embrace all children of God and welcome traditional and non-traditional households in our church family." It also claims, "We seek to provide spiritual nourishment for all members, encouraging them to follow their own spiritual pilgrimage through devotion, study and stewardship." Now, I suspect that if queried about that statement, the rector, Rev. Dr. Richard W. Murphy, might say that

St. Bede's encourages individual spiritual pilgrimage in accordance with Episcopal doctrine. But, on the other hand, the language is pretty darn open. What a wise thing to ascribe to, since, in reality, most people with church affiliations do find their own paths to God, whether that be through worship, service, nature, music, guided prayer, writing, or meditation.

Some of the more defining aspects of the congregation were revealed when I perused the bulletin inserts after the service. The prayer list was extensive, including the ill (listing, among others, Rabbi Leonard Helman—clearly this was a church with an ecumenical bent); those in prison; those with other needs; the elderly, infirm, and shut-ins; those who have died; and those traveling. The list must have included half of the congregation and its acquaintances.

Another insert announced the panel discussion of Mel Gibson's *The Passion of the Christ,* which I had read about in the paper. The invitation to this interfaith discussion concluded: "Come with an open mind and the spirit of a knowledge seeker. There is no safeguard as foolproof as education."

Even broader in its scope was an event announced in a third insert. The heading read, "Many Paths Lead to God." The Faith Alliance Festival was billed as "An event celebrating storytelling, music, and dance from Northern New Mexico's many faith traditions."

Obviously, there were significant cross-pollination opportunities among Santa Fe's worshipping communities. Was it because there was such a long history of—at first—conflict between indigenous and Spanish belief systems and—later—accommodation between those traditions? Was I seeing signs of simple acknowledgment and acceptance of differences—or actual respect and embracing of those differences?

The Passion of the Christ
MARCH 8, 2004

On March 1, I listened to a National Public Radio story about Iraqis making a pilgrimage to the southern part of their country in memory of the martyr Hussein, who had been beheaded. The pilgrims were also flagellants. I thought about the Penitent brotherhood that practices in New Mexico and wondered how many religions have branches that seek to replicate the suffering of their faith's leader. How many religions venerate a leader who suffered a gruesome death?

The story was particularly timely for coinciding with the release of Mel Gibson's movie *The Passion of the Christ*. I'd heard enough in reviews of the film to know that I wouldn't watch it. As I told a coworker who went to the movie with members of her church, "I don't like horror movies—no matter who's sponsoring them." From what I'd heard from her and the media, the overblown suffering of Christ co-opted the full story of Christ's passion and resurrection, and I didn't want to have anything to do with even indirectly supporting Gibson's brand of Christianity.

Why could Gibson not have spent his wealth making a movie about the suffering of millions of people around the world today? People who are suffering in the name of God or Allah. After all, Christ did say that whenever we feed the hungry, heal the sick, or visit those in prison, we're ministering to him.

But enough about what I think.

On the second day of my grand tour I had the opportunity to attend a panel discussion on Gibson's movie. The event was held at Temple Beth Shalom and was sponsored by the Jewish and

Christian Dialogue of Santa Fe and the Santa Fe Ministerial Alliance. The evening promised to be a way to learn more about the movie (without having to put money in Mel Gibson's pockets) and to gain some insight into how Santa Fe's clergy relate to each other.

Temple Beth Shalom is a broad, high-ceilinged, inviting space with honey-hued beams that evoke the feeling of a national park lodge. The building is modern and the interior décor minimalist: pillars, pulpit, a bit of blue and white design surrounding a Star of David. It was my first time inside a Jewish house of worship.

There was a buzz in the sanctuary that evening with people from various backgrounds seeking a place to sit and checking out the rest of the crowd. As I was arriving, the assembly had grown so large that the hosts had to remove a divider between the sanctuary and a reception room in order to expand the seating space.

As our host, Rabbi Marvin Schwab, welcomed everyone, he noted that, when he was growing up, he never saw a Christian invited to speak in the synagogue. What he didn't mention at the time was that he had just recently filled the pulpit at a Lutheran church on a Sunday when the Lutheran pastor was unavailable.

The Reverend Holly Beaumont, president of the Jewish and Christian Dialogue and the evening's moderator, asked all of us to "suspend some of your convictions" and began by listing the five guidelines for interfaith dialogue. Interfaith dialogue is not about disputation or debate (it is about hearing each other), is not about proselytizing, is not about syncretism, is not about relativism, and is not about triumphalism (that is, the belief that "our way is right and yours is wrong").

Five middle-aged white guys composed the panel: Rabbi Schwab, biblical scholar and former Catholic priest Dr. Ben Baran, Rev. Canon Dale Coleman of the Church of the Holy Faith

Episcopal, Rev. Ben Larzelere III of Christ Lutheran Church, and Rev. Richard Murphy of St. Bede's Episcopal Church.

Baran began with a lecture about the factions of Judaism during the time of Jesus and about when and how the New Testament gospels were composed. In light of critical comments about Gibson's depiction of Jews as unkempt, black-garbed evildoers with bad teeth (to paraphrase Rabbi Schwab's later comments), Baran's reminder that Jesus was a Jew was more than incidental.

Of the gospel writers (who were originally anonymous), he said, "These are artists drawing portraits, not creating snapshots." The gospels, he explained, were not written by eyewitnesses—not the historical Matthew, Mark, Luke, and John—but by second- and third-generation followers of Christ who didn't yet call themselves Christians. That fact in part is responsible for the varying accounts of the same events in Christ's life, notably his birth, passion, and resurrection. The gospels, Baran noted, were "arranged for theological motives." So, apparently, was Gibson's story of the passion of Christ.

Assorted problems with the sound system created some irritation for listeners, and as Baran's presentation stretched to and beyond a half hour, the audience grew visibly restless—eager to hear and talk about the movie rather than historical context. The fellow next to me started nervously shaking his Nike-clad foot. Nevertheless, the scholar did provide a meaningful context for understanding the biblical passion story that should have been valuable for those unfamiliar with the Christian tradition.

The discussion that followed was loosely guided by the moderator. With no particular framework, the panelists' comments tended to meander from one line of thought to another—touching now on an idea Baran had introduced, lighting for a moment on personal reactions to the movie, moving on to how each clergy member treats the passion story within his congregation.

Moderator Beaumont, for example, noted that Christ's crucifixion was "relatively mild and merciful" compared with the rampant crucifixion at the time. Instead of the three crosses mentioned in the gospels, there would have been hundreds to thousands of crosses around Jerusalem, bearing bodies and corpses in varying stages of decay—all designed to intimidate the Jews. The bottom line: Christ didn't suffer any more than any other human caught in the Roman persecution of his day.

Talk about historical context.

Rev. Coleman was the only one who actually liked the movie. He found it "very moving." Later he said, "It left me quiet, moved, in prayer." In contrast, his Episcopal colleague, Rev. Murphy, "came away quite angry and quite upset. . . . You can't isolate the passion from the resurrection and Easter."

Baran suggested that viewers allow themselves to have their understanding of the passion be corrected by the Bible—Gibson's putative source material. In contrast to the twenty excruciating minutes of torture shown on film, Mark spends half a sentence on the crucifixion: "And they crucified him, and divided his garments among them, casting lots for them, to decide what each should take" (Mark 15:24).

One of the evening's concerns was, naturally, anti-Semitism. Addressing that theme, Rev. Larzelere went off on a rather convoluted monologue about how involvement in the Jewish and Christian Dialogue has affected his preaching and how "faith is experiential." We're in agreement there; after all, it's one of the premises of this book. I struggled to follow Larzelere's train of thought; he seemed to be straining for words, as if he was trying to be theologically accurate and academically sound. At one point he mentioned something about an event in 1995 "in this temple," during which his church body, the Evangelical Lutheran Church in America, repudiated Martin Luther's anti-Semitic remarks. He then went on to tell the group that he omits derogatory words about Jews when he reads the Palm-Passion texts because there isn't time to discuss them—presumably because he lacks time to explain the context that Baran had provided that evening. Now that jolted me to attention. A Lutheran pastor altering or omitting biblical text! Well, if the gospel writers were artists bent upon tutelage, and if Gibson had the same aim, why not the well-meaning preacher who's well versed not only in biblical tradition but in the perils of decontextualized "gospel"? As Baran said at the opening of his lecture, "Words only have meaning in context."

Then Larzelere said something unexpected: "There's nothing in that movie that would make me want to become a Christian." The brutality, he argued, was inappropriate for children or young adults. He had sat in the movie theater behind a couple of children aged four or five. As the movie progressed, they sank lower and lower into their seats until he couldn't see their heads. Among his other observations were that the "Satan creature" appears only with the Jews. In his conclusion, Larzelere said that he saw the movie only out of obligation. Despite his tortuous start, something in his commentary hit the heart of his audience, including me, and he earned a hearty round of applause.

Rabbi Schwab read from several reviews of the movie, focusing on the movie's potential to incite anti-Semitism. Though Schwab understands that "This is the passion according to Mel," I doubt that the average cinema-goer would grasp that critical fact. Schwab had no solutions to the problems the movie raises, though he did seem to find some hope in a comment made to him by the pastor of a community church who said he wouldn't preach anti-Semitism because it's un-Christian.

In response to a question or comment from the audience, Murphy noted that, "We see crucifixions around us every day, in the homeless, in children seeking education . . ." and faulted the movie for failing to point to those crucifixions all around us.

Rabbi Schwab closed the discussion by pointing out that something good had come out of the controversy over Gibson's movie. In addition to the evening's interfaith gathering, his congregation was planning to host a quarterly movie night and to look at Jewish and Christian texts together in its adult education program.

I don't think it was an accident that this event was scheduled for the second day I embarked upon my own interfaith dialogue. I found hope in the fact that this group of clergy, strong in their own faith traditions, could recognize the validity of the other voices and the godly imperative of listening to others without designs of conversion—only conversation.

I had been blessed to be part of a diverse congregation. Despite our varied backgrounds, there was a feeling that we all wanted to be part of a larger body of believers—one that could dispel the darkness of division that Gibson's movie seemed intended to create.

A "New Spirituality"?
March 11, 2004

Does God change or does human understanding of God change? I'm willing to bet it's the latter. That's a bet Neale Donald Walsch has made as well.

Last Sunday, after visiting the Episcopalians, I stopped to browse at Garcia Street Books, which had a poster advertising a visit by the author of *Tomorrow's God*. Neale Donald Walsch, I learned from browsing his other books on the shelf, has written a series of books based on the premise that they're transcriptions of his "conversations with God."

The timing of the event—just as I was starting research for this project—seemed too convenient to ignore, so I revisited the bookstore the following Thursday afternoon to hear Walsch speak before he signed books. I went with the intention of hearing what someone who would use the same literary device as was employed by biblical writers would say in person and to see who else might turn out for the event.

Walsch, who appeared to be in his mid- to late sixties, was dressed in a nondescript white shirt with black trousers and black leather jacket. He wore his wavy gray hair and beard on the long side. He spoke softly. Maybe he'd worn out his voice in the previous hour with a radio interview, or maybe his voice is just soft.

He began by speaking proudly of the "worldwide movement," centered on HumanitysTeam.com, and the "worldwide following for the message" that his books had inspired. I wondered why it was HumanitysTeam.com rather than HumanitysTeam.org.

Roughly thirty-five people had gathered to hear the author. They ranged in age from twentysomething to over sixty. Though predominantly Anglo and female, the crowd included a very Santa Fe–style hipply dressed Native American male with long dark hair and a woman of Asian descent. One of the few people sitting on chairs was a woman who leaned her interlaced fingers on a stack of books in front of her, as in prayer, for most of the talk.

Walsch spoke of this being "an important moment" in our history and, though he said he didn't want to be a doomsayer, he talked of "the slow but sure erosion of our quality of life" in the past few decades, evinced by such increasingly common phenomena as metal detectors at the entrances to public schools.

With glancing references to terrorists, he pronounced, "We all want the same stuff." Hmmm, I thought. I bet there are at least a few people in other parts of the world who would disagree. If he had held a Q&A session, I would have asked him how he proposed to get his message into the hands of disaffected men and women in the Arab world—and then persuade them that his unified, de-clawed vision of spirituality was in their best interests.

A couple of times as he spoke, the rather loud *ka-ching* of the cash register interrupted him, and he turned to look in its direction, with, it seemed, annoyance. I felt like saying, "Hey, man, that's the sound that feeds you!"

Walsch wrote *New Revelations* after the September 11, 2001, attacks. His initial plan was to write a book titled *Dying with God,* but he was suffering writer's block. His publisher, who, he admitted, was paying a lot of money for the books, told him to write anything and put his name on it. Thereafter he took six days to write the first ten chapters of *New Revelations.* It took him three and a half weeks to write *Tomorrow's God.* (This book took more than six days, because it's grounded in primary research!)

Walsch's books are based on the notion that humans have mis-construed God for centuries and that the time is ripe for a new vision of God. Walsch said that when NBC's Matt Lauer asked him if he could sum up God's message in one sentence, he replied that it would be, "You've got me all wrong." Walsch, accordingly, has taken it as his mission to describe a new spirituality.

"Why am I bringing this message to Santa Fe?" he asked his audience. "To quote President Kennedy from shortly before he was killed, 'From those to whom much has been given, much is asked.'" Odd, I thought, that he didn't quote the original source of that quotation—the New Testament book of Luke. His implication seemed to be that Santa Feans have many material and other resources that they can bring to bear upon his cause.

My cynical self couldn't help thinking that he was visiting us because Santa Fe is known nationwide as a center of alternative thinkers and seekers of all stripes. In fact, Santa Fe and Taos chapters of Humanity's Team had already formed and had representatives on hand to encourage others to join them. The group's Web site states its mission as "Seeking to free humanity from the oppression of its beliefs about God, about Life, and about each other in order to create a different world." Just how it works toward that goal seems to be by encouraging those who are dissatisfied with traditional religious notions of God to join Humanity's Team study groups and events. Even though the site claims that Humanity's Team is about fostering a new spirituality rather than a new religion, any time you organize people into groups, rule-making tends to result.

To be perfectly blunt, the Web site and Humanity's Team are elements of a clever marketing strategy for publicizing and selling Walsch's books—not that there's anything wrong with that. I do, however, hope that there's a true desire to reform religion behind both the organization and the books.

In the preface to one of the books in the Conversations with God series, Walsch acknowledges that he has nothing much new to say and that he's borrowed freely from all of the world's major religions for his insights. Where he differs is in treating them more ecu-menically, it seems, and in promoting only their positive messages. He claims that there's no one way to God, and he says he's not encouraging readers to abandon or reject their faith traditions but rather to enlarge them. I had to admit that I was sympathetic to that agenda.

But then I wondered if his sincerity was just a little over the top when he got teary-eyed and choked up while delivering his parting words: "Don't think there's nothing you can do. That would be the biggest mistake."

As I walked out of the store, a woman who exited behind me asked, "What did you think?" She was tall, lanky, in her late forties, and bubbly. Her long blond hair was pulled into a puckish off-center ponytail.

I asked if she was with the bookstore. She wasn't.

I said I hadn't read any of Walsch's books. She hadn't either.

I said I'd just seen the poster, and the topic sounding intriguing, so I came out of curiosity. So had she.

Finally, I committed to an opinion: "I thought what he said was pretty benign; you couldn't argue with too much of it."

She added that everything he said was borrowed from some existing spiritual tradition, and I told her that he acknowledges that in his books. Then she noted (as I had) the irony that Walsch had quoted the Bible but attributed the words to Kennedy.

Though I was hurrying off to meet my husband for dinner, I had to ask her, "So what do you do?"

"I'm a writer," she replied with a smile and a shrug of her shoulders, "so I think about these things all the time."

First Presbyterian Church
March 14, 2004

First Presbyterian Church claims to be New Mexico's oldest Protestant church. The congregation formed in 1867, and its downtown church has been deemed historically significant. However, its worship practice wasn't as dated as I had expected.

David went with me to First Pres on the third Sunday in Lent. I wasn't expecting too much from "the frozen chosen" as I've heard Presbyterians called. It's one of the few Christian denominations for which I have never been a substitute organist. My only Sunday experience with Presbyterians had been when we visited First Pres in Boulder many years ago. The anti-gay sermon we heard that day repulsed both of us, and we never returned.

Santa Fe's First Pres was a pleasant surprise. Not only did they have greeters at the door with bulletins, but they also took considerable time at the beginning of the service to wander the sanctuary greeting each other. Unlike the more liturgical churches—Lutheran, Catholic, and Episcopal—they didn't "share the peace" by saying, "The peace of the Lord" or similar words as they shook hands or hugged each other (yes, there was even a bit of hugging going on in this Presbyterian church). Instead, they simply said, "Good morning" or "Welcome." The woman sitting next to us introduced herself by name and invited us to coffee after the service. For a moment I wondered if we'd wandered into a Lutheran church.

The sanctuary's high ceilings are crowned with New Mexican–style beams. A modern wooden cross hangs behind the choir with what look like arrow shafts sticking out from between the cross beams. I found it an attractive sanctuary, with one exception.

An American flag stood in the corner of one of the short transepts. I'd seen the flag in other Baptist and Presbyterian churches, but I'd always disliked seeing it there. The separation of church and state should go both ways. In Matthew, Christ advises the Pharisees to "Render therefore to Caesar the things that are Caesar's, and to God the things that are God's." We don't need the flag to remind us that we're American. On the contrary, church is a place where we should forget our nationality and focus on what it means for all the earth's people to be God's children.

Although their music director was out of town, the choir presented a passable rendition of a Lenten introit text sung to a German Lutheran chorale tune. (There's no denying that Lutheran hymnody has infiltrated just about every Christian denomination.) There was more hunting and gathering for notes in their anthem, "Ave Verum Corpus," by William Byrd. The twelve or fourteen members included at least four in their mid-eighties. The introit for the later service was listed as being different, which made me wonder if there were two choirs and if we'd scored the second string.

Therein lies one of the difficulties of evaluating a church based on just one service. At most churches I've been familiar with, even if the form of worship or style of music isn't different, the composition of the congregants varies between services. Often the difference is a generational one—families with children gravitating toward one service while the empty nesters and retirees compose the majority at the other. The division can be so stark that one might as well be attending two different churches.

Another pleasant surprise was that the service leader, who read the responsorial call to worship, confession, and one of the day's lessons, was a high school boy. He read well and seemed to have prepared better than many adult readers I've heard.

This Presbyterian assembly dispelled other preconceptions as well. For one, the senior pastor is a woman, with a Lutheran-sounding surname no less: Sheila Gustafson. For another, the language of their service was surprisingly modern—more modern than that used in the Episcopal liturgy.

Liturgy, literally "the work of the people," is a double-edged sword. By its familiarity and its regulated placement in the service, it confers continuity and a creates a sense of being tied to the historical church. But that same familiarity can lead to mindless repetition of the Kyrie, Gloria, Agnus Dei, and other elements in highly liturgical churches and to rote articulation of the call to worship and confession in the Presbyterian church.

But maybe this church varied the phrasing of its familiar forms frequently enough to avoid their ossification. The language of the call to confession and prayer of confession, printed in the day's service bulletin, was colloquial rather than formal:

> Call to Confession
>
> The confession of our sin before God and one another reminds us that as individual believers and as a community of faith, we do stray or turn from ways of love and justice. We believe that if we confess we shall be forgiven and freed from the burden of guilt and empowered to carry on the ministry of Christ. Therefore, with confidence in the mercy of God, let us pray together.
>
> Prayer of Confession
>
> God whose heart beats within creation, we confess our turning away from you. You give us life and freedom and we have traded it for convenience and greed. You celebrate at the birth of earth's children, and we have watched in passivity as they have

struggled and died. You ask us to care for each other, and we have been preoccupied with our personal insecurities. Forgive us Lord.

That's a far cry from the "I, a poor, miserable sinner . . ." that begins—even today—the confession in the Missouri Lutheran church that my husband was raised in. Hence, the Missouri Lutherans have earned from me the moniker Misery Lutherans. That's not to say that I dispute the fact that we've all failed to live perfect lives. It's just that God doesn't create miserable work. In contrast, the Presbyterians' confession contains an implied invitation to love and life rather than the implied threat of a vengeful God.

After the confession came a Kyrie (though it wasn't labeled that) with words and music copyrighted 1996. The three stanzas were interspersed with prayer, some of whose text seemed downright liberal: "You cry out for us to follow a way of peace, and we have supported governments that tear whole countries apart in violence and war. Help us to be strong in the face of adversity that we might seek your truth in love. Help us to care for your creation so that nothing feels outside of your embracing arms. Help us Lord."

In the children's message, Associate Pastor Matthew Davis spoke about good and bad habits. For some people, churchgoing is a habit. A good one, we could argue, but a habit nonetheless. For me, being a Lutheran would be a hard habit to break, given that Lutheran institutions and people have played such major roles in my life. Maybe that's an even stronger reason to examine my Lutheran habit by entertaining the possibility that other ways of worship have something meaningful to offer me.

Pastor Davis took his sermon theme from one of the day's scripture readings, which included the parable from Luke about a fig tree:

"A man had a fig tree planted in his vineyard; and he came seeking fruit on it and found none. And he said to the vinedresser, 'Lo, these three years I have come seeking fruit on this fig tree, and I find none. Cut it down; why should it use up the ground?' And he answered him, 'Let it alone, sir, this year also, till I dig about it and put on manure. And if it bears fruit next year, well and good; but if not, you can cut it down.' "

I paid particular attention to this little parable, for I had recently ordered a fig tree for our courtyard. I knew it was a mere "whip" that would not bear fruit the first year, but, hearing the lesson, I wondered how patient I would be with my fig tree. I hadn't ordered it for biblical reasons (fig leaves are said to have clothed Adam and Eve) but because fresh figs are second only to apricots on my lusciousness scale (I've heard that some scholars believe the "apple" in the Garden of Eden was actually an apricot).

Pastor Davis may have been reading from a contemporary translation of the Bible; whether or not he was, he hesitated and stumbled and finally substituted the word *soil* when he reached *manure* or its synonym. Unlike the high schooler, he appeared not to have rehearsed—though I know he studied the lesson, because his sermon was based on it. Instead, it seemed that, when he hit the excremental word, he was embarrassed to speak it in front of his congregation. That was a clear sign to me that he was no gardener, for well-aged manure is considered black gold for enriching garden soil. Despite my dismay at his prudery, his sermon was quite satisfactory and even helped poke another hole in my preconceptions about Presbyterians and their beliefs.

I had heard it said that Presbyterians take their good fiscal fortune as a sign that they are God's chosen people. Now, the fact that this cliché ignores the reality that there must be penurious Presbyterians should make one question such stereotypes. However, throughout history every religious group has declared in one way or another that its path is the right way to God or salvation or its equivalent, so it isn't unbelievable that this church might hold such views. But then Pastor Davis flat out declared that wealth is not a sign of God's blessing. It was almost as if the entire service had been set up to challenge every little belief I had forgotten I held about Presbyterians.

Davis said something else in his sermon that made it seem as if he'd heard about Neale Donald Walsch's recent visit. He talked about repentance as a "conversation with God." Now, whether or not that trope was intended as a counter to, or sideways gesture toward, Walsch's Conversations with God books, it struck me as an interesting way to conceive of repentance. We ask forgiveness, and we receive absolution. Short conversation, you say? Next Sunday we ask forgiveness, and we receive absolution. And the same the following Sunday. It's an ongoing, if tedious, conversation. Though Davis didn't elaborate on the idea, if I were to do so, I'd say that it's a wonderful way to imagine a relationship with God. We keep sinning, but we keep striving not to and keep admitting when we've screwed up. As we admit our failures, we ask for God's help to screw up a little less the next time. And every time, God says, "Your sins are forgiven." Of course, like any conversation in any relationship, it can be as empty or as heartfelt as we dare to make it. The only difference is that our interlocutor never changes. Never withholds.

As he prepared to give the benediction, Pastor Davis noted that we'd all had a reminder that week that we cannot control God's creation. A young mountain lion had been spotted wandering around downtown Santa Fe and had walked past the Presbyterian church on its tour of the town. All we can do, Davis said, is partake of God's creation and enjoy it.

Then he gave a benediction that sounded like a variant of the Navajo Blessing Way Prayer, but he substituted *God* for *beauty*. The middle of the Navajo prayer says, in one rendition:

With beauty before me, may I walk.
With beauty behind me, may I walk.
With beauty above me, may I walk.
With beauty below me, may I walk.
With beauty all around me, may I walk.

Whether Davis's Christian spin on this blessing was one of the formally sanctioned versions of the benediction in the Presbyterian church or a nod to the pervasiveness of Native American cultures in the area, it struck me as beautiful. Ever since I first encountered that Navajo blessing while studying "minority" literature in graduate school, I have thought that it was the most powerful, holistic, and assuring blessing I had ever heard.

The United Church of Santa Fe
March 28, 2004

The United Church of Christ (UCC) is the Pilgrim's church. David and I were familiar with it from our two years of serving, respectively, as choir director and organist for a UCC (also known as Congregational) congregation on Massachusetts' South Shore while I was in graduate school. Every Sunday morning we'd rise at six in order to make the one-hour drive from our Boston suburb to the white, New England frame church in time for choir practice and service. This schedule was especially trying for David, who usually got home around one a.m. after working the Saturday dinner shift at a popular seafood restaurant.

Our experience with that parish was mixed. The choir was small but fairly enthusiastic and included two good-hearted instrumental music teachers. The organ was a wheezing, crackling electronic "tube" contraption. I never knew when we'd have to suffer its complaints during a hymn or choir anthem.

Two circumstances precipitated our letters of resignation. One involved the organ.

One of the professional-musician choir members heard of a nearby congregation that was moving out of its building and wanting to donate its tracker organ to another congregation. All the UCC church had to do was pay for the move and then have the instrument overhauled. The UCC church had a balcony that was never used but that was just the right size for the freebie pipe organ. There would have been an initial outlay of several thousand dollars to put the organ in good working order in its new space, but after that, the church would incur only modest yearly tuning costs. The decision seemed like a no-brainer to us and to the two other professional musicians. The church's current "instrument" was really a faulty appliance that created disharmony rather than music. It should have been thrown in the landfill long before our arrival. Soon the congregation would have to shell out big bucks for some type of new instrument (even if that were another electronic organ), so the higher-value pipe organ looked like a miraculous gift. But this congregation chose to see the gift as a Trojan horse and refused to accept it.

Then there was the matter of the ubiquitous "Amen." David and I had tried to persuade the worship committee on numerous occasions that the "Amen" appearing at the end of each entry in the hymnal just wasn't musically or liturgically fitting in every case. But the committee members were incapable of seeing the value of even limited reformation if it meant straying from what was printed in their *Pilgrim Hymnal.*

Finally, we decided that making the weekly commute to such an intransigent congregation just wasn't worth the lost sleep and musical frustration. At a worship committee meeting at which we suspected we might be reprimanded or let go for making so many waves, we made a preemptive strike by presenting our letters of resignation as soon as the meeting opened.

Maybe it was the nearly two decades between that Massachusetts experience and our visit to the Santa Fe UCC church that accounts for the differences. But somehow I doubt that, even today, the New England Pilgrim assembly is worshipping the way its Santa Fe sister congregation does.

We visited on Passion Sunday. In 2004 that was more than just the Sunday before Palm Sunday on the liturgical calendar. In 2004, the actor and director Mel Gibson had seen to it that every Christian church somehow addressed the passion theme a bit differently. I doubt Gibson would have suspected that a preacher could depart so far from his bloodthirsty spectacle to celebrate the broader and more life-affirming meaning of Christ's passion. You could call it the revenge of the full gospel. But I'm getting ahead of myself.

The United Church of Santa Fe is a relatively new building, contemporary in architectural angles but giving a nod to Santa Fe style with alternating panels of glass and exposed adobe brick along one wall of the sanctuary. The spare design aesthetic carries through in the rough-hewn altar and modern wrought iron candle holders and cross. Despite the carpet, the acoustics were passable. A baby grand piano serves as the worship-leading keyboard.

When we passed through the front doors we were welcomed not only by the greeters but also by the pastor, who happened to be in the narthex. Rev. Talitha Arnold invited us to sign the guest register to get their newsletter. I said, "Maybe on our way out." (On our way out I signed only our first names. We don't need to be on any more mailing lists.)

At the eight-thirty service, at least two couples might have been lesbian couples. I remark on this because, even in liberal Boulder, I wasn't accustomed to seeing same-sex partners together in church and because Santa Fe has a reputation as having a higher-than-average percentage of gays and lesbians. Also, the church's brochure advertises that the UCC "is a progressive faith tradition . . . [that] continues to be in the vanguard of inclusiveness, welcoming all people." How wonderfully Christ-like.

Only forty people sat in the rows of padded chairs. Not even half of the chairs were full. Later, I discovered that the choir sings at the second service, so that's probably the more fully attended one. But our choice may have turned out to be a blessing in disguise, for we were treated to a superb violin and piano offertory.

Meredith Treaster, a member of the congregation, we assumed, played the "Allegro molte e con brio" from Dmitri Kabalevsky's

Violin Concerto in C Major, op. 48, accompanied by Lin Raymond, the music director and pianist. The piece was, as its title suggests, lively and even somewhat virtuosic. I'd never seen someone Meredith's age—fourteen, perhaps—perform with such professionalism, such poise, with musicality but without superfluous drama. She barely looked at the music. We were spellbound. The rest of the congregation must have been used to hearing her perform, because we seemed to be the only ones thanking her after the service. As we did, she flashed a smile exposing her colored braces.

The pianist wasn't half bad either. A few movements from Prokofiev's Visions Fugitives constituted the prelude. Knowing how capable the pianist was, I was disappointed that his hymn playing was straight from the book, without inventive introduction or embellishment. Perhaps he's improvisationally challenged, as am I—a shortcoming I blame on traditional classical piano training.

The congregational music selections were appropriate for the day and musically satisfying. For the introit—the Taize Community's version of "Ubi Caritas, et Amor"—we had just words in the bulletin. Luckily, David and I were familiar with much of the popular Taize music. Two other selections were presented the same way. For a visitor other than a well-rounded church musician, having words without music would have made it more difficult to participate in singing.

We also sang "What Wondrous Love" (Southern Harmony); a verse of a hymn set to a familiar-sounding Sacred Harp tune; "We Yearn O Christ, for Wholeness," sung to the Passion Chorale, composed by Hans Leo Hassler and arranged by J.S. Bach—more of that Lutheran music crossing denominational borders; "There Is a Balm in Gilead" (African American); and "How Can I Keep From Singing?" (Endless Song). Altogether an ecumenical mix of styles, periods, and traditions that fit seamlessly into the service. Not a dog among the choices. David and I couldn't help but sing harmony for at least the middle verses, and after the service, the woman in front of us turned to say she had enjoyed our singing.

Though there wasn't a sung version of a Kyrie or Great Thanksgiving, the general shape of the Catholic mass remained. The only disappointment was that the communion "wine" was grape juice. I suppose it was more important that the bulletin announced that "All are welcome" to share communion, "whatever this meal represents for you," as Rev. Arnold added.

There were more moments of silence in the service than we were used to. That has been one of my frustrations with Lutheran worship (at least in the many congregations I've been exposed to). We Lutherans are good at moving worship along, segueing from one piece of the service to the next; we're less good at giving people time to reflect quietly, to internalize what they've just heard or prayed or sung. Now, I don't think that I could take this desire for silent meditation to the extreme that Quakers do—I need music!—but there should be a balance.

The most unusual element of the UCC liturgy was a sort of meditative breathing exercise. Early in the service, Rev. Arnold invited the congregation to "Breathe in the peace of God. . . ." And then she breathed deeply. "Breathe in the hope that God gives. . . ." And she breathed another deep breath. "Breathe in the love that God gives. . . ."As I listened to the pastor's breathing amplified through the sound system, I thought to myself, "Now, *this* could happen only in Santa Fe!"

It made me think that we had a bit of yoga breathing infiltrating the Christian rite. Later I thought, Why not? We read and sing and talk about the "breath of God," and breath is a sign of life, so what better way to celebrate life, invigorate life, sanctify life, than by conscious, meditative breathing? Here was an element of worship that went beyond Christian ecumenism to a broader ecumenism. In retrospect, the conscious breathing strikes me as one possibly useful way to counter the tendency of Christianity to be more cerebral than visceral. Such breathing could help worshippers feel the presence of God the way that an awareness of God could potentially be as ubiquitous as every breath we breathe.

However sound the idea of meditative, congregational breathing, I wonder how it would play in Peoria.

Like St. Bede's Episcopal, the UCC church lacks a pulpit, though it does have a lectern for the reading of lessons. Standing between the altar and the front row of seats, the white-haired, fifty-something Rev. Arnold delivered the day's sermon. She was the second woman on my tour to deliver an exemplary sermon without notes.

Arnold took as her text the day's reading from Mark, telling of how Jesus had just raised Lazarus from the dead and later dined with Martha and Lazarus. Then along comes Mary with a pound of expensive ointment and anoints the feet of Jesus, thereby perfuming not only his feet but also the air that everyone was breathing. In other gospels, Mary is shown wiping Jesus' feet with her hair. In Mark, the simple anointing is sensual enough to create a highly charged, passionate scene. Of course, Judas the thief complains about the waste of money that could have been used for the poor (read, siphoned off for his own pocket). At the end of the lesson, we're told that when the chief priests heard that a great crowd of people came to see Jesus and the miraculously living Lazarus, they planned to put both men to death, because news of the miracle involving Lazarus was prompting many Jews to desert the synagogue for Jesus.

Rev. Arnold then proceeded to share with her parishioners an image of a passionate Christ that's presented throughout the gospels. In effect, she put the conventional passion—that is, the suffering and death of Christ—in the larger context of his whole life. To limit our view of Christ's passion to his death, she was saying, is not to see the whole Jesus. It's interesting, she pointed out, that Christ's passion is put in the context of—is immediately preceded by—two other passionate episodes: raising Lazarus and Mary's anointing Jesus' feet with nard—an event in which all the senses are evoked.

Then Arnold enlarged the canvass by reminding her listeners that Christ lived a passionate life his whole life—or as much of it as we know about from the gospels. He's shown loving life and people—healing them and feeding them. He's shown crying not just in the garden of Gethsemane but also at the death of a friend and upon seeing the city of Jerusalem. In the latter case, tears seem to be evoked not just by his foreknowledge of the cross that awaits him but for all the sadness in Jerusalem's past and future, she suggested.

Jesus is shown as a corporeal being who doesn't conceive of God the Father as just some disembodied know-it-all in the sky (my words, not Arnold's). Instead, when asked about the kingdom of God, he tells his followers that they can see God's kingdom in the birds and the grass and in the leavening that miraculously makes bread rise.

If the other listeners heard what I heard, they left church that morning with a sense of Christ's passion as being fuller, richer, and more hopeful than the passion image created by Mel Gibson's movie. And that's even before you factor in the resurrection—which is the whole point of the cross episode and something Gibson ignores. The picture Rev. Arnold painted was one in which Christ's suffering is one dimension of many dimensions in a passionately lived life to which all humans can relate. Yes, the final passionate episode leads to death, but that death is placed in the context, in various gospels, of Mary's anointing Jesus' feet with perfume, of Jesus instructing the disciples to wash each others' feet (I wonder where he got that idea), and with the sharing of a meal: lessons in how to care for each other.

First Baptist Church
April 4, 2004

First Baptist wins the prize for the most unusual "welcome" *chotzke*.

As congregants were greeting each other at the opening of the service, a woman passed me a nail file, saying, "Every woman likes nail files!" When I got home and dug the emery board out of my purse, I saw that—instead of a Bible verse—it held a political message on a red, white, and blue background: "Elect Ralph L. Jaramillo."

Though that gesture probably says as much about Santa Fe as it does about First Baptist Church, I still found it appalling that anyone would make such a blatant political pitch in a worship service. Remember what Christ did to the money changers he found in the temple? I suspect he'd have a similar reaction to the political influence peddlers.

First Baptist sits on Old Pecos Road, where it makes the most of being on a prime traffic route with its outdoor, live nativity scene in the week before Christmas. Other than that, I knew nothing of this church or its denomination, though I had played a few services at First Baptist Church in Boulder, which was American Baptist. Santa Fe's First Baptist is Southern Baptist. Think altar calls and "Amens."

The sanctuary's interior was more like that of a mega-Baptist church I'd been to in Denver (for a Las Vegas–style Christmas pageant) than the more conventionally ecclesiastical, Gothic structure in Boulder. Even if the stage had not been set for that evening's children's musical, the space would have resembled an auditorium more than a sacred space. Padded pews rose at an even pitch up from the altar/stage to the back of the perfectly rectangular room so that there were no unobscured views. As we stood through the prayers I made a mental note that the slope of the floors would make this a dangerous place to wear high heels, because your toenails would be pushed halfway through the toes of your shoes by the time prayers ended. The flat, painted ceiling was broken at even intervals by light fixtures and industrial-style air vents. Projectors pointed at two enormous flat screens in the front and one in the back of the room. As we entered, announcements were cycling through on the screens. Later, the screens were used to project song lyrics, the Bible lesson of the day, and various screen savers, including a cross with a crown of thorns.

Though it was Palm Sunday, there were no palms in evidence, nor was the story of Jesus riding into Jerusalem read. Instead, we got two rounds of an insipid "Hosanna" praise song. And no music to read either—even if we had wanted to join in.I apologize to those who find spiritual and musical sustenance in praise song repertoire, but I don't.

I confess that I've never been a fan of John Tesh's music, but I watched his 2003 Christmas special on PBS because it was set on the Amalfi coast. When Tesh ended with a decidedly un-Christmasy Christian praise song, I was reminded of everything I dislike about the genre. "Our God is an awesome God" was the refrain, and there wasn't much versifying wrapped around that phrase. Now, one could argue that other worship genres also lean heavily on repetition of simple texts. Some African American gospel songs are predominantly refrain-based, and several of the Taize community songs derive their power from repetition, sometimes with slight variation. But what's being repeated is usually a bit more emotionally, linguistically, and theologically rich than "Our God is an awesome God," which—despite the original meaning of "awesome"—just comes off sounding like Valley Girl–speak when paired with contemporary pop accompaniment.

So what exactly is praise music? Hard to say precisely, but in practice, it's generally sung to words on a screen rather than being presented as words and music in a book or bulletin. The lyrics are simple, often repetitive, and, based on the dozen or more examples I've been exposed to, unpoetic. It's contemporary music that doesn't derive from traditional hymnody in any apparent way.

On the subject of praise music, I once heard a Lutheran pastor ask rhetorically, "What about lament music?" He had a point, for the Bible is full of songs of lament as well as praise.

For me, praise music is like cotton candy to someone weaned on tree-ripened fruit. It's teeth-achingly sweet and artificially colored. Tree-ripened fruit, on the other hand, delivers complex flavors and textures and just the right amount of tartness to balance the fructose. And then there's the relative nutritional value.

My prejudice against praise music reveals my musical conditioning, but there's more to my views than that. I also believe that offering a steady diet of unnotated, unsophisticated praise music is a huge disservice to worshippers, especially to the young, in an age in which music education in the schools is so paltry. Instead, churches could be setting good musical examples and providing sound musical training and exposure to rich repertoire.

Even if I did like praise music, I would have found First Baptist's service unwelcoming, because no musical notes were provided for any sung element in the service. All we had were words in the bulletin and on the screens. A choir of eighteen plus two song leaders stood up front for the first three numbers: "Hosanna," "Blessed Jesus," and "Lamb of God."

Accompaniment was provided by an ensemble composed of electronic organ, piano, synthesizer, and drums. I suspected that there could be some problems with three keyboards—and there were. The piano didn't provide sufficient rhythmic leadership, which should have been its forte. The organ was practically inaudible (which may have been a blessing), while the synthesizer completely muddied the sound by providing vox humana strains that could have been more effectively produced by the organ. Then there was the drummer. David put it more bluntly than I would have: "I've never heard such an awful drummer who couldn't find the beat." In the young drummer's defense, I'd say that, without a score to read, how could he know where the verses and refrains fell or where the two microphoned song leaders would choose to ritard? At least the congregation was encouraging young musicians.

Two other musical selections rounded out the morning, and both were accompanied by canned music, complete with recorded back-up choir. A solo titled "When He Was on the Cross" was sung by a sixty-something gentleman, and just before the close of the service the song leaders sang "The Old Rugged Cross." The best way I can describe the style of these pieces is to say that they sounded like watered-down easy-listening country. (The church's new music director was performing in Branson, Missouri, the week that we visited.)

Pastor Lee Herring didn't wear a clerical robe. Nor did he use notes for his sermon. He did, however, use a microphone, which raised the decibels to my discomfort zone when he got cranked up and started shouting in his falsetto voice.

I find it difficult to write about his sermon. I don't want to sound condescending or insensitive to other worship traditions, but I admit that I found the sermon weak in spite of the pastor's strong voice.

As Pastor Herring began speaking, he invited everyone to open their Bibles to the text of the day (the only one used in the service). Most people opened one of the many Bibles in the pew holders. In fact, there were more Bibles than (unused) hymnals in the pews. The man in front of us opened his own Bible, which contained a multitude of markings.

Herring took as his text Colossians 2:13–14, which reads: "And you, who were dead in trespasses and the uncircumcision of your flesh, God made alive together with him, having forgiven us all our trespasses, having canceled the bond which stood against us with its legal demands; this he set aside, nailing it to the cross." (My translation comes from *The New Oxford Annotated Bible,* and though theirs varied slightly, the gist was the same.)

The key note throughout Herring's sermon was that Christ cancelled our sin by his death on the cross. No surprise there from a fundamentalist preacher. But there is a problem when someone takes biblical text as literally true but ignores parts of the truth. Pastor Herring began by declaring that those who don't believe in Jesus are the walking dead (that would be a majority of humankind walking the earth right now). He used as his jumping-off point the phrase "you, who were dead in trespasses." However, he never addressed the bit about "the uncircumcision of your flesh." I'm guessing that the majority of First Baptist men are uncircumcised, so how did the pastor wrestle with that bit about being "dead . . . in the uncircumcision of your flesh"? He didn't. Instead, he focused on the words "God made alive together with him."

In the course of the sermon, Pastor Herring walked into the aisles and grabbed a few hands as he spoke. (Coincidentally, the next morning I read that among the new rules and regulations for the Catholic mass is one decreeing that priests must stay at the pulpit during the sermon rather than mingling with parishioners.) Herring mentioned Mel Gibson's film *The Passion of the Christ* and opined that it wasn't necessary to see it but that it wasn't a bad movie to see either, that it wasn't anti-Semitic, and that Gibson's main message is that his hand and his sins nailed Christ to the cross. The sermon included a few anecdotes, which prompted members to laugh a bit. The fellow at the end of our pew interjected several "Amens" and other affirmations. It wasn't a bad sermon; it was just a shallow, repetitive one. It didn't struggle with the difficulties of understanding an ancient text that comes to us through historical, political, and linguistic mediation. It didn't give me anything intellectually or spiritually reviving or new to meditate on during or after the service.

The "Invitation" portion of the service, or altar call, followed the sermon and was prefaced by the pastor's explanation that receiving Christ was "as simple as ABC: Admit your sin, believe in Christ, and confess Christ as your savior." As the congregation stood to sing another musicless song, I saw one woman make her way to the stairs where the pastor stood. Simple ABC answers may be satisfying to some people, but I find such theological attitudes enfeebling and enslaving. They mask the fact that faith, like life in general, is a journey, and they ignore the fact that there is more than one way to discover and affirm one's belief in God or some other higher reality.

The bulletin proclaimed that First Baptist's purpose is "Going, Baptizing, Teaching, and Witnessing in the name of the Father, Son, and Holy Spirit according to the Commands of Christ." In contrast to other mission statements I'd seen lately, there was no word of inclusivity—of welcoming all God's children, no matter what their race, creed, or sexual orientation (in fact, their Web site made it clear that they are against homosexuality). Nor was there any hint of living out Christ's word through social justice.

The focus throughout the service—in word, song, and prayer—was on the relationship of the worshipper to Jesus Christ. To me it seemed a very selfish and self-centered theology. In the car on the way home, David admitted he hadn't been sure what to expect of the church and remarked, "It's so different from the theology and worship patterns we're used to. It's the kind of theology I find almost scary sometimes, because it's so simplistic. There's an aspect of it that's very controlling: You're bad, you're a sinner, and if you don't believe in Christ—*the way we do*—you're damned to hell."

As we were making lunch, David said that what he found scary about the theology he'd heard voiced that morning was that it seemed a small step to a potentially lethal us/them dichotomy that could be used to justify antigovernment, anti–non-Christian (maybe even anti-–non-Baptist) violence. This is not to say that I expect Pastor Herring ever preaches violence against "nonbelievers" but that the implications of his theology could be easily warped to un–Christ-like ends.

The announcements included one concerning an evangelizing trip to Thailand. New Mexican Baptists were taking along used prescription eyeglasses and a new evangelism brochure that was also available for "sharing with neighbors, waitresses, coworkers, and for sending through the mail."

I've always been uncomfortable with overt evangelizing. I happen to think that if you are a good Christian, your example will be enough to win over others who might be looking for a spiritual path, and that invitations to worship that eschew pressure tactics are better at winning true converts to a faith or denomination. However, that may just be my timid Lutheranism revealing itself. When I was accosted by American evangelists at a train station in Germany during the summer of my junior year in college, I remember being more afraid of them than of the homeless beggars, who were less aggressive.

The First Baptist sanctuary was nearly full the day we visited, the congregation seemed to respond to its pastor's sermon, and the members were friendly with each other and with us. Clearly, the church is serving the needs of its people.

My needs, however, were not met. In a seventy-five-minute service that did not include communion or formal liturgy, I had not been fed by the half-hour sermon nor the worship music. The prayers came closest to meaning anything, largely because they started with thanks for much-needed precipitation, and I'm a firm believer in giving thanks for nature's blessings.

Not to mock Pastor Herring's ABCs, but I have my own: I *admit* that I'm a musical snob, I *believe* that the quality of a church's music often reflects the sophistication of its theology, and I *confess* that I could never be a Baptist.

HOLY WEEK: LUTHERAN AND CATHOLIC
Christ Lutheran, Maundy Thursday
April 8, 2004

I had not planned to attend Holy Week services. Maybe it was the still-too-fresh memories of the marathon in previous years. I used to joke that, in our house, Holy Week was known as Hell Week. On the Monday and Tuesday following Palm Sunday, I would be practicing for the rest of the week's services and for Easter Sunday. On Wednesday we had choir rehearsal. Then there were evening services (most with the choir) on Maundy Thursday, Good Friday, and Saturday. That was all a prelude to the Easter Sunday service replete with extra choir anthems, instrumental and choir descants, rousing and technically challenging organ prelude and postlude, and perhaps a vocal solo. David, however, was feeling nostalgic for all the activity, so we decided to visit Christ Lutheran Church, hoping for something familiar during this most traditional week for Christians.

We had visited Christ Lutheran in early February on a Sunday when the pastor and organist were both out of town. Considering that we'd heard only their substitutes, we owed them a fresh visit.

We took a bulletin from the usher and chose a pew in the back third of the church, next to the choir seats. The bulletin heading was "Triduum, Maundy Thursday," but it contained no explanation of what Triduum meant, nor did the pastor provide one at the beginning of the service. Rev. Benjamin Larzelere III offered no welcome or greeting at all.

The church was roughly half full of the same mix of people we'd seen that February Sunday: grade-school acolytes, a couple of teenagers, middle-aged and older adults—including one possibly gay couple. After the organ prelude, we all sang "A Lamb Goes Uncomplaining Forth." David complained later that we had to sing all the verses of this double hymn as well as all verses of every other hymn. Even before the service began, he had pronounced the hymn selections "dogs," to which I retorted, "Who's behaving badly this time?" (I had complained about the substitute organist's tempos and instinctively sang a fraction of a second ahead of the played beat, which drives David crazy. "You're not going to make them play faster," he always says when I fall into this pattern.) At least the regular organist switched up the registrations a bit and alternated melody and harmony for A and B phrases of her hymn introductions.

After the gathering hymn came the confession and forgiveness. Rev. Larzelere pronounced the absolution to the whole congregation, at the end of which at least half of the congregants crossed themselves when they spoke the names of the Trinity. Then Larzelere offered a laying-on-of-hands absolution to those who wished to come up to the altar rail. Most did. We didn't. If the first absolution didn't take, why would the second?

Then followed prayer, the Exodus story of the Passover, a psalm, a reading from Corinthians recounting the Last Supper, the gospel reading of the Last Supper from John, and the sermon. "Worship is a drama," Rev. Larzelere proclaimed. He proceeded to describe that drama as moving from gathering to storytelling to meal to sending. All the parts are necessary, he said. Then, finally, he explained that Triduum is the three-part, three-day service from Thursday through Saturday's Easter vigil. As church musicians, David and I knew that walking in, but if we hadn't, we might have thought we were about to worship in a foreign language.

Worship has often been understood as drama, and many worshippers attend services regularly because the familiar rituals are sustaining and create a feeling of security. However, this was the most undramatic service I'd attended in a long while. Whereas our Boulder church had offered foot washing as well as the Eucharist to worshippers on Maundy Thursday—something that Christ in the day's readings adjures his followers to do, just as he tells them to remember him when sharing bread and wine—this congregation offered only communion. Reenacting the foot washing made the gospel come to life and had been very moving for many who participated in it. It was worship as spiritual drama.

The most dramatic element of the service was the singing of two psalms by one of the choir members. He was well-rehearsed, enunciated clearly, and was, well, dramatic. I might otherwise have thought his performance was melodramatic, but in the context of an otherwise flat service, his contribution was welcome.

Another element of the service that put us in a grumpy mood was the congregation's use of the third setting of the Lutheran liturgy. *The Lutheran Book of Worship* includes three musical settings of the liturgy. Of all the Lutheran churches in which I've worshipped or worked since 1978, when this worship book was introduced, I've only heard the third setting used twice, and then only for short periods, like during Lent—as if in penance (which Lutherans don't even believe in). After one trial use of that setting during Lent at our Boulder church, we permanently ignored it. There's no question that, from a musical standpoint, it's a dud.

During the prelude to communion—known as the Great Thanksgiving—there was more crossing of chests and even bowing to the altar. In fact, there was more crossing and genuflecting than I'd seen in most Roman Catholic churches. It's all part of what we'd call "high church." I wouldn't have been surprised to smell incense. Christ Lutheran offers such high church that it sacrifices connection with this worshipper's life. Maybe Christ Lutheran's members enjoy the formality, but I felt sorry for the young people who would grow up knowing only their home church's expression of Lutheranism.

When, during their confusing communion parade, David and I rose to follow close behind the people in front of us (so as not to screw up the traffic pattern), the young man serving as usher next to our pew looked at us in horror or fear that we should rise without his bidding. I thought for a moment that the burly lad might push David back into the pew.

"The only bright spot," said David after the service, "was that little girl." While assisting with communion, the eight-year-old acolyte with a blond braid flashed a smile at someone kneeling at the communion rail. David saw her smile and it made him smile. She caught him grinning and threw an even wider smile back at him. Like Jesus said, it's the little children who know best how to enter the kingdom of heaven.

"If you can't say something nice, don't say anything at all" isn't a motto that works for writers. We have to tell the bad with the good or we're not worth our words. However, I derive no pleasure from commenting on what I perceive as disappointing worship—especially in a Lutheran church. I would love to find good worship everywhere.

Even though the service we attended fell flat for us, we don't dislike the pastor. Rev. Larzelere is a warm person, very well respected in the community, active in various ecumenical efforts, and beloved by his parishioners. However, those qualities didn't shine through in the service. Our experience made me wonder how much pastors shape their congregations' worship tastes and how much congregations' predilections attract certain kinds of pastors.

Good Friday Morning
April 9, 2004

"That cathedral is packed!" David exclaimed as we were driving down Interstate 25 toward Albuquerque on Good Friday morning.

"You mean that *casino?*" I corrected him.

But his slip of the tongue was apt. I think gamblers must gamble because they *believe* they'll be lucky. Because they have *faith* that if they give, they'll receive.

The Sandia casino's parking lot was jammed at nine a.m. on the holiest of Fridays for Christians. Now, I admit that making a shopping expedition is probably not a lot more holy than gambling, but we were in search of food and hiking maps rather than a quick buck.

I'm not against gambling per se, but it does sadden me to see all the Indian pueblo–owned casinos up and down the New Mexico interstate. I'm all for native enterprise, but in such a poor state, it seems that the proliferation of casinos demonstrates a lack of imagination to envision more life-sustaining forms of employment and entertainment.

On our drive we saw a few late pilgrims walking on the shoulder of the interstate, making their way to the sanctuario at Chimayo—a nearly 200-year-old shrine in a tiny town north of Santa Fe. During Holy Week, New Mexico police suspend upholding the law that forbids foot traffic on interstate highways. Instead, cops positioned at intervals along the main roads leading to Chimayo keep an eye open for people in need of assistance.

The pilgrimage is an annual Holy Week event in which twenty thousand to thirty thousand people would participate this year. Some walked from as far away as Albuquerque, while others, including my Lutheran sister-in-law and brother-in-law, would walk just the last few miles to the small chapel. Some carried crosses. Some said the rosary the whole way. Some made the pilgrimage in memory of deceased loved ones or those serving in Iraq. Many believe that the chapel's holy dirt (dug nearby and blessed by a priest) has curative powers. The chapel was built by a man named Bernardo Abeyta, who in the early 1800s saw a glow on a hill near his home during Holy Week. He dug up the dirt on the spot he'd seen glowing and found a six-foot crucifix. That crucifix hangs in the sanctuario today.

Santa Maria de la Paz Catholic Community, Good Friday, April 9, 2004

Now, *this* was drama. Everything that Rev. Larzelere spoke of on Thursday was brought to life the following night: gathering, story, meal, and sending—worship as drama.

But the drama wasn't at the Lutheran church. Instead, it was at Santa Fe's newest Roman Catholic church, Santa Maria de la Paz. We went there because one of David's coworkers sings tenor in the choir at Santa Maria de la Paz and because we'd heard it was a popular, progressive Catholic church. We took with us David's sister Diane. Her husband, Tom, was presiding over a service at the Presbyterian church in Albuquerque where he was serving as interim pastor.

The building, of New Mexican pueblo style, looks grand from the moment you approach it. Walking up to the front doors, you look up to the bell tower, which stretches into the sky as high as the cathedral's towers. Inside, the sanctuary is large without appearing cavernous. Banked pews form a horseshoe around the altar. The décor is understated Santa Fe Spanish—tinwork chandeliers and pine pews in whose backs Southwestern designs have been carved out. The nave has a lofty tongue-and-groove ceiling with vigas. In spite of lower ceilings above the flanking sides of the congregation, choir acoustics are decent.

We arrived just minutes before seven, and the place was nearly filled to capacity. There were no bulletins, so we just took our seats toward the back of a side section.

The service began with an explanation of how the confirmation class would present in mime the story of the passion. The woman who was their director told those unfamiliar with the parish's clown ministry that the practice dates back to at least the tenth century and that the aim is not so much entertainment as instruction, a way to bring biblical stories to life. After she provided an interpretation of the cast's makeup and dress, the service proper began with a procession of the officiants. As the priest reached the altar, he instructed us to kneel. The three of us—and a few others, also obviously visitors—reached for the kneelers. There were none. We knelt directly on the concrete floor. After a minute or so of silence, we were told to rise, and the cycle of prayers, lessons, and responsorial songs began. Women as well as men, Anglo and Hispanic, read and led the singing.

Though the church has both an organ and grand piano, with the exception of the choir's anthem—a setting of "Adoramus te"—there was no instrumental accompaniment of singing. I missed the keyboards but thought the a capella choice fitting for the service. The absence of notes did, however, irk me. As a visitor, I had to rely on my ear to pick up both words and melody for all the responsive psalms and songs. Only the communion hymn, "What Wondrous Love," was in the hymnal, and that one I could sing mostly from memory.

As a group of white-faced, black-garbed teenagers read the passion story, more than a hundred of their cohorts enacted the story of Judas' betrayal, Jesus before Ciaphus and Pilate, the walk to Calvary, the nailing to the cross, Christ's death, and Joseph of Arimathea arranging for the body's burial in a private tomb. In the background, a sound track of classical music played. Not once did anyone act inappropriately. The mimes were well rehearsed and worshipful. The narrator and the voice of Jesus were female, as was the actor depicting Pilate. Mimes, as the director had told us at the beginning of the service, are neither male nor female. As the young man playing Christ "hung" on the cross, the sound and lighting system created a grand thunder and lightning storm and an image of lightning was projected on the wall at the front of the chancel. The only disruption of the drama came when a few people took flash photos of the scene. As Christ's body was carried out of the sanctuary to be "buried," the projected image changed to the head of Christ wearing a crown of thorns.

After the enactment of the gospel, the priest, a lightly bearded Hispanic probably in his late thirties, gave the homily. He thanked the confirmands for their hard work and good job (saying that Mel Gibson had better watch out for the competition) and led a lengthy round of applause for them. Then he told how, if you put all the descriptions of Christ together in a composite drawing, you'd end up with a man of modest stature and unremarkable features. He did not dwell on Christ's suffering and passion, however. Nor did he browbeat his listeners with the theology of the crucifixion. His closing message was the most poignant yet hope-filled Good Friday message I can remember hearing: "There is no fear that the cross can't heal."

He repeated that assurance, calmly, without histrionics, and spoke to his parishioners about their own fears and our fears for the world. "There is no fear that the cross can't heal." Whatever one's views on the war in Iraq, I can't imagine anyone not having some fears about its outcome. Whatever one's economic or health status, I can't imagine anyone without some deep, dark fears. Instead of focusing on how Christ died for our sin, he focused on the root of sin: fear. It was an inspired message. And the drama was in the pairing of his calm assurance with images of the cross surrounding the sanctuary and with the teenagers' enactment of the familiar passion story.

Speaking without notes, the priest had moved around the front of the altar to face all sides of the congregation as he spoke. He didn't look awkward in doing so, nor did he pander to the parishioners. There wasn't a trace of self-dramatization or showmanship. Nevertheless, if he were going to follow the new edict of his church, come December (when the rule was to go into effect), he'd have to stay put in the pulpit while delivering his sermons. Such rules imposed across all churches are simply misguided, for in the worship space of Santa Maria de la Paz, the priest's movement clearly made his sermon more personal and more real. Given the configuration of the sanctuary, a pulpit sermon would not reach all parishioners in the same way.

The Eucharist, accompanied by one congregational hymn and the choir anthem, followed the sermon. As the priest ended the Great Thanksgiving by saying, "Lord, I am not worthy to receive you, but only say the word and I shall be healed," a synapse fired: *That's* where I remembered those words from; when Rev. Larzelere had spoken them the previous night, I knew I hadn't heard them in a Lutheran church before; I'd heard them while serving as organist in a Catholic church.

The choir of roughly twenty-five did an honorable job with the anthem and a couple of descants. They sang a cappella for the most part, in tune, and the four or five soloists had fine voices. Comparing them with other Catholic choirs I'd heard, I could understand why David's coworker would make an hour's commute every Wednesday and Sunday to sing with them.

I suspect that the format for the prayers of the day was a bit different than it would have been in a Sunday service, but it reminded me that liturgy is the *work* of the people. After each intercession we were instructed to kneel as we sang a short verse in Spanish and English, "Lord, listen to my prayer." Then we rose for the next intercession. We started counting intercessions at about number six. I think there were a dozen. Down to the floor to sing, up to listen, knee bones ground by concrete, thighs pulled by standing. There were prayers for the church, for those in public office, for the congregation, and even a prayer for the Jewish people, asking that they remain faithful to their covenants. I wondered if that last one had been in the published prayers of the day or if it had been added by the priest in response to the controversy over Gibson's movie.

The service ended with the veneration of the cross. The priest and a deacon carried the crucifix on which the artist's rendering of Christ had been covered by a robe. At each of the three sides of the congregation, they pulled back a section of the robe. Then the confirmation class processed out, two by two, carrying the stations of the cross, which had stood in a semicircle behind the congregation during the service. My sister-in-law told us that the retablos decorating the crosses had been created by a famous artist and were the congregation's pride and joy. After all the crosses had left the sanctuary, the crucifix from the church's altar cross remained in front of the altar, held by the priest and deacon. While some of us left the sanctuary in silence, others walked into its center to touch or kiss the cross.

It was the most welcoming Catholic service I'd ever witnessed. I'd attended mass at several Catholic churches and cathedrals while on vacations and had been organist at the largest Catholic church in Boulder for two and a half years. In the prayers, although there was an intercession for all believers to be united in one church, the language didn't specify the Roman Catholic church. It was probably implied in the minds of the prayer writers, but as a non-Catholic, I chose to see a loophole instead of a noose. The invitation to communion welcomed all who believe, not all who were Catholic, so we took the priest at his word and joined the procession of those who received the sacrament, which was just a wafer.

I think I understand one of the reasons that Santa Maria de la Paz is such a popular community. Though I don't make drama the measure of a worship experience, for those who do, these Catholics definitely have the edge over Lutherans—at least on festival days.

Cathedral Church of
St. Francis of Assisi
Easter, April 11, 2004

The choice of venue for Easter Sunday was obvious. When you're playing church tourist and you have a cathedral in town, that's where you go.

Archbishop Jean Baptiste Lamy—made famous in literature by Willa Cather's novel *Death Comes for the Archbishop*—laid the cornerstone of Santa Fe's cathedral in 1869, and the church is named for the city's patron saint. Architecturally, the Cathedral of St. Francis of Assisi is described as French-Romanesque. Its sandstone was quarried not far from where we live, near the hamlet of Lamy, which was, no surprise, named after the bishop. The interior has been updated over the years, from the post–Vatican II altar to the more recent and unique baptismal font. The "font" sits in the center aisle in the midst of congregational pews and could best be described as an art installation consisting of black marble, burnished metal, bubbling water, and a pool.

Stone pillars flank the nave, and in both side aisles hang colorful retablos of the stations of the cross. A retablo reaching almost to the ceiling sits behind the altar and depicts various saints and biblical figures. *Retablo* literally means "behind the altar" and is a form of Mexican devotional art that typically consists of oil painting on tin or wood.

It snowed Easter eve and Easter Sunday, making Santa Fe look as if it were enjoying a white Christmas rather than a spring green Easter. As we drove into town for the ten a.m. "Pontifical" mass at which the archbishop was presiding, we listened to Robert Shaw's recording of J.S. Bach's Mass in B minor. It's hard at such times not to feel just a little pride in the fact that the most extensive and most gorgeous Latin mass setting was written by a Lutheran.

This might be a good time for a few words on the relationship between the Roman Catholic and Lutheran churches. The idea of the Reformation was literally reformation. Just as Jesus didn't set out to create "Christianity," but rather a reformation of Judaism, Martin Luther, a Catholic priest, didn't set out to create a religion called "Lutheranism," but rather a reformation of what he saw as untenable practices in the Roman Catholic Church. However, established religions have a tendency to resist reformation, which forces those who can no longer practice their inherited faith hypocritically to form new worship traditions.

One indication that Lutheranism derives so directly from Catholicism is that Lutherans have retained the structure of the mass in Sunday worship: Kyrie, Gloria, lessons, gospel, creed, Great Thanksgiving, Agnus Dei, and postcommunion prayer or canticle. Most Lutheran churches celebrate the Eucharist each Sunday, as Catholics do at each mass.

What's interesting is how, over the centuries, Lutherans have influenced Catholic worship. Most obvious is the use of hymns and hymn tunes composed by Lutheran composers that one can find in Catholic hymnals—from Bach to Marty Haugen.

For both those reasons, when David and I worship in a Catholic church, when we listen to the songs and words of the liturgy, we feel quite at home. It's only when a priest preaches about certain elements of Catholic doctrine that we're jarred into the reality that we're not in a Lutheran sanctuary.

It's hard not to be impressed by Santa Fe's cathedral when you enter to the strains of a harp and see before you the enormous and colorful altarpiece. Lit by lamps and sunlight, the gold background of the altarpiece figures glowed on Easter morning. Easter lilies and calla lilies decorated the altar and niches. The cross was draped in white. A new Paschal candle held center stage, rising four feet above its stand.

We were glad we'd arrived at the cathedral a half hour before the English mass began. By nine-forty, the space was at two-thirds capacity, and the crowd would eventually fill the main sanctuary and balcony as well as the adjacent chapel, leaving the latest to lean against pillars.

Though we were wished a Happy Easter as we entered, I was sorry we weren't offered a bulletin—a not uncommon omission in Catholic churches. On the way out, I saw an usher with a sheaf of them and asked for one, but the bulletin turned out to be just that: a bulletin of announcements and events in the life of the church. On the back were more than thirty classified ads for local businesses. What I really had hoped to see was a listing of the day's special music.

As we were seated, the choir of nearly thirty, under the direction of an attractive and very pregnant thirty-something director, sang a contemporary setting of the words, "Take, O take me as I am . . . set your seal upon my heart." Amazingly, the congregation was quiet enough that everyone could hear the choral prelude.

At fifteen minutes before service time, the choir director welcomed visitors as well as parishioners and led us all through a rehearsal for worship that started with the "common song" of the day. After one pass through a portion of the sung liturgy, led by her stunning voice, she cajoled, "It's Easter, let's sing! Let's try it again." She also explained that the cantors would lead the singing and would gesture to indicate when the congregation was to join in. Clearly, she cared about the quality of worship and knew how to encourage participation.

In spite of the smart decision to hold a congregational rehearsal (necessary because there were no printed words or music for any of the liturgy), few in the congregation actually sung during the service, not even the David Haas setting of Psalm 118, with its infectious Alleluia refrain, or the Haas Gloria. All ages were well represented at this service and all were equally timid when it came to singing. The three young children in the pew in front of us never opened their mouths. I, in contrast, remember singing in church long before I could read. My dearest wish as a preschooler was to be old enough to sing in the children's choir.

After the congregational rehearsal was another choir anthem, sounding suspiciously like Handel, accompanied by piano, trumpet, and timpani; then an organ prelude. During the service we would hear these instruments plus the harp, flute, guitar, xylophone, and bells. It was a celebratory ensemble for a festival day. The richness of the music matched the splendor of the space and the grand procession of priests, acolytes with candles, and new converts that made its way up the center aisle during the singing of "Jesus Christ Is Risen Today." In fact, the procession was so lengthy that we had to sing two extra verses before all those officiating were settled on the altar platform.

Both men and women led singing, read lessons, and served communion, but there would be only one gender delivering the sermon and blessing the sacrament of Holy Communion.

Archbishop Michael Sheehan began his sermon with a joke: After Joseph of Arimathea had given his new tomb to Jesus, he went home to his wife and said, "I have some good news and some bad news." She replied, "Give me the bad news first." Joseph said, "I've given my beautiful new tomb to Jesus. But the good news is that he'll give it back in three days." He got a mild chuckle from the congregation.

From there the homily devolved into what David called a seven-minute "policy sermon." After an endorsement of Mel Gibson's film, the archbishop, crowned by his miter, thanked God for the twenty-five new converts who had been baptized at the cathedral the previous night. (It's tradition in the Christian church, especially in the Roman Catholic Church, to baptize new believers at the Easter Vigil service.) Then he acknowledged that we humans "are always seeking happiness. That's the way God built us. But we're often seeking it in the wrong places." Roman Catholics, he said, should seek happiness by following Jesus and the teachings of the church. If they did, there would be, he claimed, no adultery, no unwanted pregnancies, no abortions . . . no sexual abuse of minors by priests as there was *"years ago"* (emphasis mine), there would be fewer crimes and drug addictions. "Be faithful, and God will be faithful to you," he concluded.

Next we stood while the priests circled the sanctuary, blessing congregants with holy water while the choir and soloist sang an arrangement of the African American "Wade in the Water." The offertory anthem was a pop/gospel-style setting of text concerning the resurrection.

When we kneeled for the Great Thanksgiving, I was grateful that this church supplied kneelers. We took the communion wafer but passed on the common cup. There was something moving about standing during the communion hymn and then being part of the streams of believers receiving communion at several stations in an over-full house of worship.

If you're Catholic, you're probably saying, "Why is this Lutheran taking communion in a Catholic church? She's not allowed." Well, what can the pope do, excommunicate me? Seriously, though, I take communion when I'm not expressly forbidden to do so, knowing that some priests in some parishes are more or less accommodating of communing non-Catholic Christians. When I went through confirmation class I was taught that the sacrament of communion was made holy not by the hand of the person who served it but by Christ, who gave it for all believers. It doesn't matter whether the individual blessing the bread and wine is a saint, a pedophile, or a wife beater, the sacrament remains sacred to the believer who receives it. Nor do I recognize any church's authority to withhold bread and wine from anyone who desires it.

Easter mass concluded with an unfamiliar Alleluia hymn (and we thought we knew all the Easter repertoire) and Handel's "Halleluiah Chorus" sung by the choir.

After the Handel, as the keyboardist moved from the piano to the organ console to play two postludes, the choir director let out a big sigh of relief and began disassembling the sound system, lowering microphone stands, and removing microphones for storage. David and I looked at each other and remembered how that had always been our chore at the end of a service. That afternoon I decided to send the director a thank-you note, because few people understand just how much time, talent, and energy go into creating the perfect musical mood for a festival service—or any other service.

On the drive home, the CD serendipitously hit Bach's "Et resurrexit" section of the Mass in B Minor.

The following day, Easter Monday, *The New York Times* ran a story titled, "Kerry Attends Easter Services and Receives Holy Communion." Big deal, I thought. He's Catholic. Well, it turns out that last fall the U.S. Conference of Catholic Bishops had a meeting to discuss how they should treat Catholic politicians, such as Kerry, who claim to be personally against abortion but who support abortion rights in their role as legislators. (Someone needs to remind the bishops that elected officials are supposed to represent the people who elect them, not just themselves.) The bishops hadn't yet decided what they should do but had explored various penalties, including withholding communion and, ultimately, excommunication. How can any church withhold the *gifts* of God from the people of God?

To quote the *Times:* "Archbishop Sean P. O'Malley of Boston has not explicitly said Mr. Kerry could not take communion but he has suggested that Catholic politicians whose political views contradict Catholic teaching should abstain, saying they 'shouldn't dare come to communion.'" Excuse me, but there's a vas deferens (to resurrect a truly tasteless but fitting high school pun) between holding a "view" and acting in a way that the Catholic church finds immoral. I'm thinking here of the actions of more than a few priests, Boston archdiocese priests infamous among them, who engaged in not only immoral but illegal sexual practices that were clearly against the teachings of the Roman Catholic Church. However, I don't recall the bishops threatening to withhold communion, let alone threatening excommunication, for any of the priests accused of those unspeakable acts.

All I can say to Senator Kerry and other Catholics who may find themselves in his boat is, I'm sure the Evangelical Lutheran Church of America would welcome you. You'll find all the familiar parts of the mass, an open communion table, and—often—better music and sermons.

HINDUISM
APRIL 2004

One conviction I've held firmly as long as I can remember is that God—whoever or whatever that creative power is—is far greater than any human power to understand the divine. Despite every religion's attempts and every believer's struggles to define and characterize God—to codify what God desires or demands of believers—as human constructs they're doomed to failure. Our minds are too weak, our imagination too narrow, our fears too deep to embrace the full possibilities of God's reality and what it could mean to be people of God.

At the same time I find it quite plausible that the divine could have entered human history through the prophets and Jesus of Nazareth and Buddha and Mohammed. It also seems perfectly understandable that different cultures would have developed religious belief systems in keeping with their social and political histories. Like it or not, religion has been an integral part of civic life in one way or another in most civilizations.

From my North American Lutheran perspective, I want to believe that religious tolerance and religious freedom are self-evident values that can help ensure civic and worldwide peace. Trouble is, much of the world doesn't agree. Take, for example, some Hindus.

Two days after Easter I read in the local paper a story reprinted from *The Washington Post* about American religious scholars who faced attacks as a result of writing about the Hindu faith. One of the scholars commented that she felt the criticism was coming from "zealots" who hold that non-Hindus have no right to speak about the religion at all. As with all religions, it's the hard-liners, the intolerant, who seem to be on the battle lines inciting violence of one sort or another. Traditionally, Hinduism has been a fairly tolerant religion.

From what I've seen, it's ultimately fear, not faith, that under-girds zealots—in North America and elsewhere. Fear that someone else may have a glimmer of what God is and intends—something that they have missed, which could mean they're "doomed." Fear that they can't predict the final outcome of their existence. Fear that someone will disagree with them and ridicule them. Fear that some-one will proclaim that another religion is the right religion and therefore the zealot's religion must be banned or the believer killed. Fear that adherents of other religions may experience more joy and happiness.

The religioustolerance.org Web site told me that that Hinduism isn't a unified religion with a single founder, theology, morality, or organizational body, so I knew that, probably more than other wor-ship communities, whatever Hindu gathering we had in Santa Fe could not be taken as representative. The Web site also explained that Hinduism is the world's third-largest and its oldest religion, so I thought I'd better include it on my tour, even though it's clearly not the third-largest in Santa Fe. Then I read the story about the Hindu zealots.

Just as a female bar-hopper might walk past a bar outside of which she found a large crowd of inebriated males offering verbal insults to all female passersby, I bypassed the Hindu gathering. Santa Fe Hindus may bear no resemblance to militant Hindus, but why take a chance? After all, this wasn't intended as an investigative reporting assignment.

My nonexperience of Hinduism led to the realization that any religion or congregation that develops a reputation for inspiring fear and for using fear to silence anyone outside its circle from comment-ing on it wasn't a religion I'd want anything to do with.

Unfortunately, that attitude only inspires more ignorance, more intolerance, and more fear.

St. John's United Methodist Church
April 25, 2004

The big surprise was that this Methodist church sounded Baptist. As I listened to the pastors' inflections, the style of preaching, the "Lord, we just . . ." refrain in prayers, and incidental "Amens" rising from the pews, I couldn't help thinking of that famous mixed-denomination couple, the Clintons. Former President Bill Clinton, a Baptist, and Senator Hillary Rodham Clinton, a Methodist, might both have felt at home in this congregation.

My experience of Methodism was limited. During college, I served as a substitute organist for two weeks at a Methodist church in a small Minnesota town. Other than sliding off the highway on a frigid, icy Sunday morning en route to the church, my strongest memory of that gig is of the music director telling me, when I arrived at the church to practice, "Now, we Methodists take our hymns at a lively tempo—not like the Lutherans." I don't know what Lutheran churches she'd been in, but they certainly hadn't been any I'd played for. Upon hearing her implied challenge, I vowed to adopt tempi that would have those Methodists gasping for air.

As I absorbed the atmosphere of Santa Fe's flagship Methodist congregation, I reminded myself that regional and local predilections can account for a wide range of worship practices within any given denomination. I'd somehow always associated Methodists with the North and Baptists with the South, but here I was hearing a Southern echo in the male associate pastor's voice and in the female senior pastor's speech.

While I took a seat in the rear of the sanctuary, I overheard Rev. Namiqa Shipman tell already-seated parishioners that the earlier service had become the more heavily attended one—a pattern that could be seen across the denomination, she explained. When the service started, the room was not quite half full, with roughly two hundred worshippers. Ten were in the choir, which had only two men. Seven played the handbell preludes.

The handbell ensemble was quite accomplished and played without a director. Their ranks included three young adults and two retirees. Titles of the preludes, whose tunes I didn't recognize, weren't printed in the bulletin; the pieces seemed to be simply occasional music.

Visitors were asked to raise their hands so they could be presented with a small gift. We were told—though not in the words I use here—that our pew neighbors would rat us out if we didn't raise our hands, so I complied under duress. The gift was a macramé cross pinned to a brochure listing the church's program and service information. After a welcome, we were invited to "pass the peace of Jesus Christ," though rather than saying, "The peace of the Lord be with you," as is common in Lutheran and Catholic churches, most folks simply said, "Good morning."

Methodists are light on formal liturgy. Though there was no Kyrie, we did sing a Gloria. The service did not include the Eucharist, and from the standpoint of service length, that was a good thing.

The old-time opening hymn "Christ for the World We Sing" was accompanied by an electronic organ. Poor acoustics may have been partially responsible for the lackluster singing. Or members may have been even more bored with the tune than I was. Unfortunately, the music didn't improve. The choir's presentation of "Savior Like a Shepherd Lead Us" was embellished by piano but not artfully arranged for the twentieth, let alone the twenty-first century. Other congregational hymns—"What a Friend We Have in Jesus" and "Rescue the Perishing"—might be called chestnuts by the kind or war horses by the cruel.

After the opening hymn came the "Children's Moment," which consisted of readings by several middle-schoolers who portrayed the disciples at the Last Supper. Now, that's just strange, I thought, to present this story three weeks *after* Easter, rather than during the chronologically appropriate time in the church year. If you're going to observe Christmas and Easter, at least help children learn the correct order of the main events in Christ's life.

Next, a representative from the Gideon Society, which had been meeting in Santa Fe that week, made a presentation. He talked about the organization's volunteer structure, the number of Bibles distributed, and told a few anecdotes about people "receiving Jesus Christ as their personal savior."

The language we use in talking about faith matters enormously. Distrust anyone who claims otherwise. For me, the phrase "receive Christ as your personal savior" is loaded with troublesome overtones. I've never heard it in a Lutheran church; we're not publicly demonstrative, and we tend to keep "personal" faith private. I associate the phrase with evangelists, who imply that "accepting Jesus Christ as your personal savior" involves believing precisely what the proselytizer believes, not—as the words *say*—believing what Christ has revealed to the individual believer. Furthermore, the editor in me dislikes the phrase's redundancy: If I accept Christ as "my" savior, "personal" is superfluous—a rhetorical flourish for those who speak the code of fundamentalist Christianity.

When we reached sermon time, Rev. Shipman announced that the day's sermon would be a little different. She then launched into a story about how a young couple with three children had appeared at the church office on Friday, claiming that they were on an evangelism trip. When the couple said the family sang, Rev. Shipman challenged them to sing, and the "angelic voices" that rose attracted people who had been engaged in various activities throughout the church building that day. The African American father said he had a congestive heart condition and that they were trying to get back to their home in Jacksonville, Florida, for medical care. The white mother said the children's instruments had been stolen from their van while they were in Denver.

As she introduced the Hill Family Trio—two girls and their brother—Rev. Shipman reiterated that St. John's was the only church in town that had opened its doors to the family.

Finally, the service got some good singing. Taking the lead on "Amazing Grace," the six-year-old girl created more sound than the entire congregation had on the opening hymn. Her eight-year-old brother and nine-year-old sister sang classic gospel harmonies behind her. Their father tried to pump up the congregation before the second song with "Amens" and with talk about the children's singing being "biblical testimony that God is still alive and in charge." The children followed with a swaying and finger-snapping rendition of "God Is There" complete with some improv sermonizing by the boy. The congregation thanked them with applause and a standing ovation. I wonder how much the Hill family collected with their postservice freewill offering.

The clock read well past noon when Rev. Shipman gave what she called the *Reader's Digest* version of her sermon. Moving out of the pulpit, she delivered a message based on Jesus' injunction to his disciples to "Feed my sheep . . . tend my sheep . . . feed my sheep." Again I felt as if I were in a Baptist church, as the majority of her words were spoken in italic or boldface. Overemphasis, as I used to tell undergraduate writers, results in no emphasis at all.

Lest it seem that I found nothing laudable about this congregation, I should mention that its dedication to community service was impressive. Rev. Shipman announced that, for the recent Cropwalk, their church had collected $1,500 and that two-thirds of that had been raised by the junior high group.

St. John's service emphasis is appealing because it reaches beyond the congregation and its denomination and doesn't necessarily involve proselytizing. To be something more than a social club or self-serving community, any Christian church, it seems to me, needs to step beyond its walls and beyond "its kind" to serve those in need.

Religious Society of Friends
May 2, 2004

It was a quintessential spring morning in Santa Fe. The clear air was crisp but held the promise that I'd be wearing shorts by noon. As we walked down one-lane Canyon Road—famous for its blocks of galleries and specialty shops—most of the traffic seemed to be headed toward a popular breakfast spot. Our attention was focused on the leafing progress of various trees and especially the many lilacs in full bloom. Santa Fe's alkaline soil is hospitable to lilacs, which grow in many of the city's older neighborhoods.

Our destination was a historic adobe in the middle of gallery row that now houses the Santa Fe Religious Society of Friends—better known as the Quakers. It's an unlikely location for the meeting place of a group best known for its stances on conscientious objection to military service and its advocacy of a simple lifestyle, for Canyon Road boasts some of the most expensive real estate in town and is in the business of selling high-priced art, food, and clothing to those with substantial discretionary income.

We entered through a gate that opened into an archway whose walls had weathered enough to expose the adobe underneath its stucco. A sign in the first doorway directed us to the rear entrance and informed us that Friends should be aware that some Friends might have a sensitivity to fragrances. That was at least the third time I'd encountered such a sign in public places—churches, a doctor's office, and a workout studio. My reaction is always testy: How am I supposed to know that I could be encountering fragrance-sensitive people before I visit a new place? Am I to alter my personal hygiene routine in the off chance that someone might be there who may sneeze if they get too close to me?

The walkway led to an enclosed, charmingly overgrown garden. The room off the garden was a small efficiency kitchen that led into a library and then the building's former living room, now the meeting room. Rooms off to the side seemed to be used for children's and arts activities.

Inside the main room, a small card on the seats read:

> You are entering a Quaker Meeting for Worship. In silence we seek connections with God and the inspiration of the Inner Light. Sometimes we are moved to share an experience, an insight, or a message. We customarily stand to speak. We try to give messages that are brief, sincere, and that come from the heart. After each spoken ministry we pause for a period of silence.

We sat in a rear row on padded brown folding chairs. Five people were already sitting in silence. Seating for forty was arranged in a square, facing toward an open center. Straight ahead of us was the mullioned living room window, draped just high enough to obscure the street traffic. Above the muslin, lilacs swayed in the breeze. Though all was quiet below the dark vigas of the low-ceilinged room, outside birds chattered and cars roared two yards beyond the window.

I tried to determine *how* Quakers worshipped quietly. The two women sitting in front of us, later joined by a third, barely moved a muscle. A forty-something woman wearing a fleece top and travel pants had her eyes open most of the time and shifted position a lot, stretched her arms and back, and even left for the restroom after twenty minutes. With her mouth slightly open and jaw released, she seemed relaxed. Next to her on the side bench sat a fifty-something fellow with curly, graying hair. His eyes were closed and his brow was furrowed—except when he seemed to nod off as his head rocked back to rest against the wall.

I empathized with the woman who stretched. With no rising or kneeling, there was no opportunity for circulation during the hour.

About forty-five minutes into the meeting, a couple in their thirties and their two young sons entered the room and sat on the stair next to us. Their three-year-old, dressed in cowboy boots and straw cowboy hat, didn't speak but did fidget, which prompted sotto voce reprimands from his father.

No one spoke. At the end of the hour, we rose in silence, gathered in the center to hold hands in silence for a moment, and then the regulars welcomed us and made a few announcements. They said that this meeting was the smaller one and that people spoke more at the eleven o'clock meeting.

As we stood in the Santa Fe circle, I felt overdressed even though I'd have been underdressed for some churches. I was the only one wearing lip gloss, mascara, and dress shoes. It turned out that the woman in fleece was visiting with her partner from Seattle. The young couple had recently moved to the neighborhood. With us as visitors, that left only half the attendees for regulars. They were friendly but not pushy. We were all asked to introduce ourselves, but only first names were used.

No offering was collected, nor was money spoken of. I wondered how the community collected funds. Even if the building was owned outright, there'd still be taxes, utilities, and basic upkeep.

With no text to focus on, I had let my mind wonder about how Quakers became Quakers and how they determined what they believe without a formal, "denominationally sanctioned" doctrine. The absence of doctrine didn't strike me as necessarily bad. The only inkling of the Friends' belief position was indicated by a simple poster propped in a corner that read: "Have you left enough space in your life for the way to open?" Good question. Good question for any believer.

It had often struck me that mainline Christian worship provides little or no opportunity for meaningful meditation or silent prayer—for the ways that one could most likely have a truly personal relationship with God that's unmediated by the words, beliefs, and biases of preachers, hymn writers, and rule-makers. It had always been my contention that those who ask, "Do you have a personal relationship with Jesus Christ?" are precisely the people who don't want that relationship to be personal at all. Rather, they want it to be public and to be defined in ways that their group sanctions.

I also prayed for my mother-in-law's health and that she would find a way to make a decision about moving to more appropriate housing. I prayed for those in government and public service and asked that they be given the courage to say no to superiors who ask them to do things that are contrary to this country's founding principles. I asked for peace in the Middle East.

But what, I wondered, was the point of *group* silent prayer? If there's no group music-making, no group praise, no group sharing of a meal, why gather? The meeting didn't feel like worship to me even though I could appreciate the discipline of setting aside time to pray and meditate and open oneself to the light or the way. Even though I didn't leave with a sense of joy or discovery or with something to ponder in the coming week, I was glad the Friends offered a place of quiet: a place in which one is invited to listen to that "still, small voice."

Other than to make bookkeeping simple for the administrators of organized religion, why should any of us have to restrict ourselves to membership in or affiliation with just one body of believers? If I'm a child of God, surely God can recognize me whether I'm singing with the Lutherans or sitting silently with the Quakers.

On the way home, I asked David what he had been thinking about during our hour of quiet. He said he'd mainly been thinking about golf; he'd walked in his mind some of his favorite courses. He had a golf date for that afternoon, so it was natural for him to focus on the game. Though he hadn't been thinking "religious" thoughts, he was meditating, relaxing, and appreciating something he enjoys about life.

He must have been thinking a little bit about other matters, though, because later he asked, "Weren't the Quakers founded by those seeking religious freedom?" Then he wondered aloud, "Will this become another country that people leave in order to seek religious freedom?"

CHRISTIAN LIFE FELLOWSHIP, ASSEMBLY OF GOD
MAY 9, 2004

And now for something completely different from the Quakers. The moment I walked into the Christian Life Fellowship hall, I thought I was at a rock concert. The tunes being rehearsed were clearly praise music, and the decibel level was closer to concert level than worship level.

Musically, this band was an improvement over the Baptist ensemble we'd heard a few weeks earlier. The lead and bass guitar players, synthesizer player, conga drummer, and drum kit drummer played rhythmically and in tune. In fact, during the service, the drummer was seriously rockin'. A trio of singers backed up the lead vocalist and guitarist, who wore a microphone hooked over his ear like a pop star.

From the street, the adobe-colored metal walls of this Assembly of God could lead one to easily mistake the building for an industrial warehouse. Inside, acoustic tiles cover the ceiling, and brownish-orange carpet covers the floor, stage, and five full-width steps leading up to the stage. Just before the service began, someone placed boxes of facial tissue at intervals along the second stair. Did they have an altar call at which parishioners routinely broke down?

Banners lining the side walls read, "Holy Ghost Fire," "Jesus Divino," He Is Worthy," "Let It Reign, Reign, Reign," "Champion of Heaven," A People of Prayer," and "Power in the Blood." The wide wall behind the band was painted baby blue. When the projection screen used for song lyrics was raised up, a large archway and a nondescript cross were revealed. An American flag and another flag I couldn't identify stood in stands on the stage.

As I waited for the service to begin, I browsed through the handouts. A trifold brochure contained announcements, mission statement, staff roster, and a panel for notes. A "Pastor's Care Card" solicited name, contact information, and guest information as well as prayer requests. It offered options for getting more information and four check-off circles for "My Decision Today": I am committing my life to Christ, I want to be water baptized, I am renewing my commitment to Christ, and Please enroll me in the next: Pastor's Newcomers Class/Special Group. (Visitors were promised a special gift bag, prepared by the pastor's wife, if they filled out the card and gave it to one of the ladies as we left the service. I didn't take advantage of this special offer.)

Another insert announced a series of classes for codependent women and chemically dependent men. The sheet advertising the Royal Rangers program for boys—designed for "Reaching, Teaching, & Keeping Boys for Christ"—made it look like an Assembly of God version of Boy Scouts.

And then there was a sheet resembling one we'd seen at the Baptist church, with blanks to be filled in during the sermon, whose theme was "Paint Me a Picture of a Godly Mother (Woman and Wife)." Eight points were to be made, apparently, all concerning the qualities that a godly mother would have.

None of the handouts provided an outline of the service, let alone service music, so I knew I was in for highly unliturgical worship. Though the pastor made reference to the communion table at one point, no communion was served on Mother's Day.

After a welcome reading by Associate Pastor Pablo Cerquera, we were invited to stand for song. We stood for twenty-seven minutes without a break, through five praise songs. Toward the end of the singing marathon, a few older and younger members of the congregation sat in the padded pews. A handful of people, mostly women, held their hands above their heads during the singing.

Only the words to the songs were projected on the screen behind the musicians, and though the music featured predictably repetitious and unpoetic lyrics, at least the musical style was less Grand Ole Opry than what I'd heard in the Baptist church. That's not to say that I joined in the singing. Once again, the absence of musical notes made for an exclusionary newcomer's experience. Though I occasionally tapped my foot on the floor or my hands on the back of the pew in front of me, I did not participate in hand clapping. I noticed that not everyone was equally adept at rhythmic clapping, but the only woman in a hat had rhythm, and she shook a pair of maracas from time to time.

The songs had titles like "Let the River Run" and "Sing for Joy," but they were a far cry from such soulful and musically inspired cognates as the African American "Wade in the Water" and Beethoven's "Hymn to Joy." Then there was the questionable, from my point of view, theology espoused in some of the lyrics. The line, "You [God] alone are good" struck a particularly sour note with me, because it implies that we are not good in any way. If we have no good in us, then what's the point of worshipping or even of believing in a loving God, if such a God can find no good in us?

Though I'd heard complaints in Lutheran churches about late-comers, this congregation set records for lateness. When the service began at eight-thirty, roughly sixty people were in the pews. By the time the singing concluded, there were double that number, including a family that came in and sat next to me more than a half hour into the service. Maybe they didn't like praise music either.

Pastor Marcus McClain had a few words to say after the singing ended and then asked us to greet each other, which we did. Before the offering was collected, one of the elders offered a mini sermon about teaching children to give, by example and by insisting that the children give. He did, however, say something I'd never heard any-where else: "If you're a visitor, don't feel obligated to give." It was a rather refreshing comment that suggested one could take the church for a test drive before making a down payment. Nevertheless, I put my standard visitor's bill in the blue velvet money bag as it was passed.

All the mothers were given a small book titled *Whisper a Prayer for Mom* before the two dozen children distributing them were sent to the children's program. Then Pastor McClain warmed into his sermon, which he referred to as "the next twenty-five minutes"—which stretched to fifty-five. That made for a service lasting an hour and forty minutes.

It took me several days to sit down and write about the sermon. Ultimately, I decided that the less said the better about what I had heard and how I felt about what I heard. I decided to stay above ad hominem attacks even though I was tempted to make them.

During the sermon I took notes openly, because the handouts sanctioned doing so. And, although I disagreed with much of what the preacher said, I have to give the church credit for encouraging note taking during the sermon. Just as it does in a schoolroom, note taking helps the otherwise passive listener focus on the message and remember it.

The pastor's text was 2 Kings 4:8–37, and from that, he derived a message that "A Godly mother will have a giving, perceptive, con-tented, genuine, strong, believing, persistent, and reverent spirit." Now, there's nothing offensive on the surface of that. I did find it offensive, however, when he claimed that mothers and women in general have lost their spirit of contentment and "are raging around the world when God says to return to your homes . . . and find your contentment there." If that's not an antifeminist invective, I don't know what is. His "raging" comment could only be taken as inflam-matory. And where exactly does God say to women today to "return to your homes"? Barefoot and pregnant, it seems, is the only acceptable role for women in this church.

Instead of celebrating women and mothers for their immense and varied contributions to the world and to the spiritual lives of those around them, the pastor used the occasion of Mother's Day to attack women who believe differently than he about what God put them on Earth to do. Although he had eight points to make, the sermon seemed more like a pretext for personal asides that demonized anyone who held views contrary to his.

He spoke of a California women's health club whose male owner gives money to antiabortion causes, and he ridiculed those who criticize the owner's actions.

He railed against the Sandoval County clerk granting marriage licenses to homosexuals, and encouraged support for the federal Marriage Amendment.

He asked, "Where in the Sam Hill was [sic] you on Thursday for the National Day of Prayer? . . . We've got to get outside the walls and into the marketplace."

With each attack his baritone voice rose higher in pitch and the words came out of his mouth as if they were written in boldface type. Each time he slid into attack mode he'd conclude by saying, "I know I got off track." But he was clearly enjoying the fact that he had, as witnessed by his admission that the diatribe against homosexual marriage wasn't "in my notes, but I feel *good* right now!" And then he did a little twisty happy dance behind his pulpit.

The denomination's Web site told me that it was born of a religious revival in the late 1800s. Its doctrinal standards and positions on social issues are what most would consider politically conservative and even xenophobic, prohibiting, as they do, any church member from dating an "unbeliever." The site acknowledged the necessity of birth control for some people at some times but did not grant the same understanding to abortion.

I've always found it sadly ironic that antiabortionists scream about the immorality of "killing an unborn child," yet you don't see them holding pacifist views in general. To them it seems acceptable to kill full-grown human beings in other countries or, for some of the more militant, to kill adults in this country who perform abortions or who defend a woman's right to an abortion.

It's hard for me to face the fact that people who go by the name of Christian can hold views so antithetical to everything Christ stood for and did in his own life. Perhaps it's inevitable for each group that organizes under a different religious banner to define church doctrine in a way that justifies that group's beliefs. Maybe I should simply celebrate the fact that this country allows such religious pluralism. Yet I can't leave it at that, for in some communities of faith I see the potential for self-justifying hatred of those who are, or who think, differently.

So, what to do? Violence isn't an acceptable or effective answer. Counterarguments don't persuade when one's interlocutor has a closed mind. Prayer seems so passive and paltry a response—unless, of course, you believe that prayer has the power to change the world and the people in it.

First Church of Christ, Scientist, May 23, 2004

Although I lived in Boston for six years while I was in graduate school, I never visited the Mother Church of the Church of Christ, Scientist, even though it was an architectural landmark and its Mapparium was one of the city's many tourist destinations. I knew a bit about the denomination from undergraduate religion classes and from reading American history. As a young feminist, I found the idea of a denomination "discovered and founded" by a woman—one that proclaimed God "Mother and Father"—appealing. Even so, I was skeptical of the church's claims to spiritual healing. That was before the publication of scientific studies showing that prayer can help in the healing process.

I was aware of, but had never read, Mary Baker Eddy's most famous book, *Science and Health with Key to the Scriptures*. I'd seen, but never entered, Christian Science reading rooms. More than two thousand miles from the Atlantic shore, where the denomination was founded, I set foot in a Christian Science church for the first time, with no idea what to expect.

Two women stood outside the door, and one greeted me, but there was no one at the door to the sanctuary with a bulletin, so I took a seat two-thirds of the way back on the organ side. A middle-aged male organist was playing a quiet prelude on the electronic organ. I suspected that, given the size of the space, most service music was subdued.

Padded pews in orangey yellow circa 1970, carpeted floor, dark altar in a raised chancel, acoustic-tiled ceiling partially camouflaged by dark squared-off vigas, Spanish-influenced metalwork pendant light fixtures—most of the typical fittings for a Santa Fe church. Except that there was no cross.

The only adornment of the space consisted of an enormous hosta plant in front of the altar and three gold-painted inscriptions on the front walls. From left to right they were Christ's words that "the truth shall set you free"; "God is love"; and a saying from Mary Baker Eddy to the effect that divine love always has been and always will be sufficient for humanity. The emphasis on a God of love was welcoming.

As people took their seats, I watched a seventy-something woman standing at the front pew and smiling as people walked in. I wondered if she was the presiding pastor, but when the service began, it was led by a man in his forties and a different elder woman. I have no idea what the first woman's function was.

The congregation seemed a fair cross section of Santa Feans, judging by their choice of dress, which ranged from cargo pants to a white suit topped by an ivory straw hat. The younger ones were in Sunday School at service time, so it was hard to tell how family oriented the congregation was.

After a brief welcome, the male leader invited us to sing, but before we did, he read the first verse of the hymn. For the second hymn, he read all the way through all five verses before the organist played the hymn—all the way through—and then we sang. The second hymn was one written by the "discoverer and founder of Christian Science," Mary Baker Eddy, and set to music by John Stainer. The text was clunky, to be kind, with forced rhyme and such archaic language as "ayont." (Once home, I had to haul out my *Oxford English Dictionary* and its magnifying glass to learn that *ayont* means "beyond; on the other side of.") The music wasn't melodious either.

The final hymn was set to St. Hilda, a somewhat familiar tune to me, but the words were from the Christian Science tradition. By this point in the service I was so irked by the fact that the woman sitting behind me invariably sang behind the beat that I stopped singing myself and leafed through the hymnal's index. Only one in maybe twenty-five listings was familiar, and even then they'd often been given a Scientist spin. The original "Rock of Ages, cleft for me" became "Rock of Ages, Truth Divine" under the hand of Christian Scientist editors.

Before the sermon, a female soloist sang an arrangement of the Twenty-Third Psalm. The only other music was an organ interlude during collection of the offering. I wouldn't be spiritually sustained by a diet of Christian Science worship music.

For a church that puts a lot of stock in prayer, the service was rather thin on it. We began with a silent prayer and then a spoken Lord's Prayer, with each phrase followed by the Christian Science interpretation of it. There must have been some other first-time visitors, because I heard a couple of voices on the other side of the aisle about to carry on with the familiar prayer just as the male leader began the Scientist commentary on each phrase. His gloss didn't add any insight, and it messed up the prayer's rhythm.

At the start of the service, we were welcomed to "this healing service," but there were no prayers of healing, no laying on of hands, and no talk of healing. I was disappointed.

The only other congregation participation came with a responsive reading of psalm text. Rather than reading all or part of a single psalm, we read parts of three psalms, whose verses were stacked on top of each other as if they belonged to the same one. The editor in me did not approve. When we got to the excerpts from Psalm 34 that read in part, "O taste and see that the Lord is good," I longed to hear one of the lovely musical settings of that text. Actually, I would have settled for communal reading with a natural cadence. Why is it that some congregations affect a stilted, three-word-limit rhythm when they read aloud as a group?

Nor could I find sustenance in the "sermon." The male leader explained that in the Christian Science church, the sermon consists of readings from the Bible and readings from the Christian Science textbook, free of human interpretation. Well, my critical mind carped, that means that the only interpretation of the Bible allowed within these walls is the interpretation of one woman who died a century ago but who established her reading as the only right reading. That's as silly as what I'd heard a Benedictine monk declare in *The Name of the Rose,* which I'd watched on TV the night before. In the movie, an Inquisition-era cleric declares that there is no progress in knowledge—just recapitulation.

The ostensible theme of the day was "soul and body." For at least a half hour, the male and female service leaders read their texts. I can't even call them Bible passages, because they were so varied and short as to create a muddle. Though I tried to pay attention in the beginning—to find a thread of a theme—I soon gave up. Among the Bible's strengths are its narrative, poetic, and accretive tropes—none of which was able to shine through because of the grab-bag of texts chosen for the day. (And who, I wondered, chooses the readings? With no ordained clergy, there still must be some "authority" choosing the lectionary.) The Christian Science texts were no more coherent to my ear than the biblical ones. I watched the reader flip back and forth and back and forth in his book to read one and then another and yet another couple-sentence commentary.

If there was a theme in the Christian Science readings, the one that got through to me was that humans are spirit, *not* matter. I'm totally in favor of celebrating God's presence as spirit in each human being, but don't go telling me that matter isn't real, because I bleed when cut, just as Christ bled when nailed to the cross. What do Christian Scientists do with that stunningly material and visceral *suffering* of Christ on the cross? I couldn't buy into their dichotomy of spirit and body. Most humans have tended to emphasize the material over the spiritual when it comes to every aspect of religion and health. Point taken. But there's nothing scientific about ignoring the reality of matter. Where is the church that recognizes and celebrates integration of body and spirit?

Overall, Christian Science struck me as an ossified religion—at least from a worship standpoint. The hymnal was copyright 1932. Bible readings were from the King James version. The message was stuck in the late nineteenth century, in the words of Mary Baker Eddy. I wondered if the format of the service varied at all with the liturgical year celebrated by other Christian denominations.

The Mother Church's Web site proclaims that Christian Science is practiced by people belonging to all sorts of faiths. That would suggest that one can hold to Mary Baker Eddy's teachings about spiritual healing yet be a practicing Catholic or a Buddhist or a Pentecostal. (Somehow, I doubt that all of those other traditions would approve of the religious pluralism.) Yet the Web site and the magazine I found in the pew talked about membership in the Christian Science church, and membership in one church usually implies membership in only that church, so just how inclusionary is it?

The experience left me with mixed emotions about the Christian Science spiritual path. On the one hand, if all the sanctioned texts are unchangeable, at least parishioners would be spared the kind of personalized, politicized statements on current events that I endured at the Assembly of God church. On the other hand, it was deadly dull. Maybe their Wednesday evening gatherings, which include testimony, are where church really happens and where healing and the spirit are fully felt.

Though I find myself sympathetic to the church's impulse to reclaim the healing mission of Christ and the early church, I can't ignore that I live in the twenty-first century and that, if I'm going to be part of a community of believers, I want to be part of a dialogue about what it means to be the church today.

UNITY SANTA FE
JUNE 6, 2004

In a more sarcastic mood, I might call Unity Santa Fe a church of Peace and Love for aging counterculturists. But though there was a definite baby boomer element in the church (including Rev. Brendalyn Batchelor), there were also young children, thirty-somethings, and a smattering of elderly members, including a couple who were at least in their late eighties. Though mostly Anglo, the congregation included a few Hispanics and maybe even a Native American the Sunday that I visited.

My labeling isn't entirely misrepresentative, though, as evidenced by the bulletin cover, which imposed over the Unity symbol of a dove in a circle the words "Peace, Wisdom, Love." But wait: Those really were Christ's values, even if they're counterculture values as well.

I was happy to see a bulletin, after being starved for a worship outline at the previous few churches I'd visited. At Unity we received more reading material than we could absorb during the service.

The exterior of the new Unity building, which sits at the edge of Las Campanas—one of the most affluent Santa Fe developments, looks like a church but is understated in its white paint and two-tiered, crossless steeple. Inside, the sanctuary was dimly lit, but sunlight entered through small, high-set windows. Elegant banners depicting the apostles hung on the walls.

We were welcomed by Rev. Batchelor, sans clerical garb, who wore a microphone wrapped around her head that made her look like a customer service representative. She led everyone in reading the church's vision statement, which is the closest the church comes to anything resembling a creed: "Unity Santa Fe is a vibrant spiritual community that celebrates the oneness and divinity of all creation." Then we read the mission statement: "Our mission is to raise consciousness, transform lives, heal the planet."

Next, Consuelo, the music leader, invited us to sing the opening song, "Day by Day." Yup, *that* "Day by Day." Consuelo added tambourine rhythm to the pianist's jazzy accompaniment. In fact, my suspicion that Russ was really a lounge pianist was confirmed later in the service when it was mentioned that he'd just returned from accompanying Judy Collins on her tour.

Luckily, "Day by Day" is such a pop classic that we didn't miss the notes, but none of the other service music came with notes either—just words beamed to the back of the altar wall via overhead projector.

The day's worship leader, a Barbara Eden look-alike, led us through the rest of the service up to the sermon. Several announcements were made; most concerned classes on self-improvement. When first-timers were asked to raise their hands, we did so and were applauded along with the several other visitors who were given information packets.

The special music was an Aaron Copeland piece titled "The Promise of Living," from his opera *The Tender Land,* sung by mezzo-soprano Natalie Campbell, wife of the pianist. The text was worshipful and Natalie's delivery won her applause. All the regulars followed this solo by singing "Our Thoughts Are Prayers"—a simultaneously comforting and scary thought that fit with what I was hearing throughout the morning about the mind/body/spirit connection and our ability to help manifest our desires.

I saw no cross anywhere in the sanctuary, and the one brief Bible reading, from Emmet Fox's version of the Sermon on the Mount, was only loosely related to the minister's sermon, which meandered a bit too long (the service ran almost an hour and a half) given its fairly simple message. A fellow two rows in front of me with graying curls may have thought so as well, because his head and shoulders were slumped over in such a way that he could only have been snoozing.

More than anything, the sermon seemed to be an overview of Unity principles and positions—whose antidogmatism certainly appeals to me. Unity's openness to the idea that there is more than one way to God probably makes it one of the most tolerant religious organizations. Rev. Batchelor commented that Unity doesn't care if a Unity pastor decides he or she would really be more comfortable as a Buddhist. The denomination's attitude, as spelled out in one of the many handouts for visitors, is that you should take what's useful to you from Unity and may even belong to another denomination at the same time.

An active prayer life seems to be one of Unity's strengths and one of its appealing aspects. Though I missed the spoken petitions that are common in other Christian services, I appreciated Unity's silent prayer format. At Unity I realized that prayer is easier to get serious about when you can relax into it, as we were led to do during the service.

We also were asked to fill out an answered prayer/prayer request sheet, which we put in a basket with our offerings later in the service. The act of writing down those prayer details helps focus your mind on what you're grateful for and what your best self truly desires. After the service I noticed that the bulletin explained how those slips are used. The prayers "are held in prayer" at Unity Santa Fe for thirty days and then are held in prayer for another thirty days at Silent Unity, the denomination's 24/7 prayer service. I had not signed my name or address, as the form suggested, but I was glad nonetheless that I'd registered gratitude for finding Reiki (an energy-healing technique) and that I'd requested healing.

Everything was humming along comfortably until we stood to sing the Lord's Prayer to a hackneyed tune. Once again, I knew the melody, but this time I wished I hadn't. It seemed odd that such an otherwise progressive church would use such tired music. Then, for a whiplash back into the present, we had a second solo, this piece written by the pianist.

Unity calls the offering portion of its service the Prosperity Blessing. One row after another stood and processed to the front of the sanctuary to deposit prayer slips and envelopes and to light a candle and place it in a dish of salt. Why this ritual? The only explanation given was that "You are the light of the world and you are the salt of the earth." More words without music were projected during this time, and the regulars sang the songs as the whole congregation joined hands in a circle around the perimeter of the worship space. The last one, "The Prayer of St. Francis," we knew.

Then pastor and congregation spoke the prayer of protection: "The light of God surrounds me; The love of God enfolds me; The power of God protects me; The presence of God watches over me. Wherever I am, God is!" What they called "Holy hugs or handshakes" followed.

At the close of service, visitors were told, "If you liked it, come back!" No guilt trip, no hard sell, no pushing for our names even when we shook the pastor's hand.

On the way home, I asked David what he'd thought of the service. His response was, "It was a bit like group therapy. It seemed to be for affluent people who don't have any other worries. It was almost 100 percent nonscriptural." And, as I'd anticipated, the music "bugged" him: "I don't like singing the Lord's Prayer—I don't like that music."

I had to admit that my preconceptions of Unity were that it was a pretty self-centered theology and loosely Christian, a conclusion I'd drawn from random comments overheard from a few women in Boulder who attended the Unity church there. They talked about their "intentions" and professional success, and they made it seem that Unity had a system for making one's personal wishes come true.

One aspect that contributed to this sense in Santa Fe was that there were no intercessions for anyone other than those present—no prayers for world peace or for the community. I see nothing wrong with praying that one's best dreams come true, but most religions also promote care for others and their well-being. Maybe it was just an atypical Sunday in that respect.

The affirming aspect of the overall message—that the spirit of God is within each one of us rather than God being some anthropomorphized guy in the sky or some ethereal entity—was refreshing. The message may have been one of self-improvement, but it was self-improvement by following "Divine Wisdom" rather than "God's will." The difference is more than just semantic.

Maybe it was because of my training as an editor that I mentally shuddered each time Rev. Batchelor used the phrase "do ourselves consciously." Now, "do" is a highly malleable verb that often serves when no other will. Nevertheless, "doing myself" is just not an acceptable use of the verb. Do *what* with ourselves consciously? Maybe it's also because in common parlance, "doing" when linked with a person, has violent or vulgar connotations. Why doesn't it suffice to say "Live consciously"?

In defense of at least the idea behind the "do ourselves consciously" phrase, I did have the sense that this was a community of people who were soulful Christians—more than just social Christians or doctrinal Christians. Let me explain what I mean by those last two terms, as I've been more or less both at times.

Social Christians are those who attend a church for a variety of reasons that have more to do with being physically present in a particular place at a particular time than with their souls. They may attend out of habit, out of a sense of obligation to other family members, out of a desire to be affiliated with current or potential business contacts, or because they enjoy the concertlike or theaterlike experience of worship or the congregation's extra-worship activities. I see nothing wrong with those motives, except that they exclude the attendee's spiritual needs (even if those are unexamined or unacknowledged).

Doctrinal Christians (who may also be social Christians) may be said to attend church out of fear as much as faith. They hope that if they do what the church tells them, or at least attend church regularly, they will be "saved"—whatever that means to them. They may enjoy aspects of worship or the prescribed religious sacraments and rites, but they don't evince much interest in expanding their soul's possibilities. I'm not sitting in judgment of such people. After all, our culture doesn't provide much incentive to attend to one's soul in an individual way.

Though there may have been social and doctrinal reasons for some of the members' attendance, the tenor of the service suggested that people were there because it was a safe and supportive place to nurture their soul's growth, a community in which the nature of their relationship with the divine wouldn't be limited by some power-hungry leader's insistence that there is one right way to be in relationship with God. Though the service affirmed God's presence within each life, it also promoted humility by acknowledging that everyone there hadn't achieved perfection but was "doing themselves consciously."

Unity supplied the most fulsome visitor's information packet I'd ever seen. I suppose the church feels that it's worthwhile because Unity isn't as familiar to the average person as Catholicism or Methodism. One brochure outlined what Unity is and stands for. I was surprised to find that it's over a century old. I suspect that one of the most troublesome claims for mainline Christians would be this one: "UNITY proclaims the divinity of Jesus, but goes further and asserts that all people are children of God and therefore divine in nature. We are not human beings having a spiritual experience; rather, we are spiritual beings having a human experience for soul growth." If that isn't empowering and inspiring one's highest self, I don't know what is. To play Unity advocate for a moment, if we are made in God's image and are God's children, that means we must share God's divine nature—but that's one logical step that otherwise biblical literalists don't seem willing to make.

A brochure titled "The Adventure Called Unity" by Charles R. Fillmore (grandson of the founder) explains the organization's beliefs. Another explains the work of the 24/7 Silent Unity prayer ministry. Emmet Fox's "The Golden Key," a treatise on prayer first published in 1931, encourages positive prayer, in which one avoids thinking about the trouble one is in and instead thinks about God.

"A Unity View of New Age and New Thought" places Unity firmly in the Christian camp as opposed to aligning it with some of the more recent New Age practices. Of most interest to me, especially as I'd recently read Elaine Pagel's excellent book on early Christianity, *Beyond Belief,* was this brochure's explanation of Unity as a type of "primitive Christianity"—a way of life based on what Jesus taught rather than what later institutional doctrine and dogma imposed on believers.

As in the political realm, so too in the religious realm: No one likes living under a dictatorship, even if it's run by a "benign" fascist. That's because dictators rule by fear—of physical death or of hell. I experienced no fear factor at Unity. Instead, I felt hope and encouragement to be our best selves by living up to the divine spark within us.

Unitarian Universalist Congregation of Santa Fe
June 13, 2004

Unitarian Universalists—or "UUs," as the Reverend Dr. Stephen H. Furrer called them—are one of the most unorganized of organized religions in that they have no set creed or dogma. Instead, according to the day's bulletin, they honor the teachings of "the great prophets and teachers of humanity in every age and tradition," which likely accounts for the absence of any cross in the sanctuary. Further independence derives from the fact that policy is set by individual congregations. I can see how Unitarian Universalism might be liberating for those who chafed under dogma- and ritual-laden religious training earlier in their lives. To paraphrase this congregation's mission statement, it's a liberal religious community that's open to the search for truth and justice and that supports spiritual growth, education, and self-empowerment. All good things that I'm in favor of. As a *worship* experience, however, the service I attended offered little spiritual sustenance, and I don't think that was directly a result of the total absence of the words "God," "Christ," and "Jesus" (probably even "Spirit," though I can't trust memory on that one).

Granted, it may have been an atypical Sunday. "Bizarre" would not be too strong an adjective for a service that included a sermon on same-sex marriage and Broadway music by Steven Sondheim for prelude, musical meditation, and offertory. The Sondheim served as a preview of the following weekend's dinner theater at the church. The sermon topic was prompted by a vote later that morning on whether the congregation should support same-sex marriage.

Though lacking formal liturgy and a meal, there was an order to the service that included a few rituals: a drum to summon worshippers into the sanctuary, a chime to begin service, lighting of a chalice, and lighting candles for joy or sorrow. With the exception of a reference to a passage in Judges, there were no Bible readings. Instead, texts for the day centered on the sermon theme and included Walt Whitman's poem "When I Heard at the Close of the Day" and the Massachusetts Chief Justice's ruling on same-sex marriage. Not your typical lectionary.

Then there are my wine, women, and song criteria. Because UUs aren't formally Christian, there's no Eucharist. Though the pastor was male, I had a sense that women are honored in the denomination, given its basic beliefs. (A subsequent visit to the UU's Web site reminded me that Universalists were the first denomination to ordain women.) As for the non-Sondheim song, of the two hymns we sung, only one tune, "Truro," was familiar but had been paired with unfamiliar text. Singing was tepid. I confess again that for me music is one of the most important elements of a worship service. It's the one thing that, to a greater degree than rite or words, can transcend our human limitations by giving expression to our longings and prayers, by putting us in a meditative frame of mind, by helping us glorify the divine.

As the offering basket went around, I heard a lot of noise, which I first took to mean that these were paltry givers. Afterward, I noticed a bulletin announcement that change goes into a fund for community social justice. Just shows that you have to be totally in the know before you judge.

Standing behind the pulpit in his tan-colored suit, full beard, and ponytail, Rev. Furrer delivered what was probably the most political sermon I've heard outside of a Catholic church. However, the difference was that I agreed with his politics. And the social politics espoused were defended on the basis of love and justice rather than fear and control. In advocating for the acknowledgment of same-sex marriage, he used the specific example of the Massachusetts couple, Julie and Hillary Goodrich, who brought suit in their home state. He happens to know the couple and their daughter, Annie, and so was able to make the case personal rather than abstract. His defense hinged on defining marriage by function rather than form—not by what families look like but by what they do. By that standard, the Goodwins have a sound, happy family. He also pointed out that neoconservatives who rail against same-sex marriage spend far less time and effort seeking to improve the state of heterosexual marriage—how it functions—and tend to downplay both the difficulties within heterosexual marriage, including abuse and divorce, and the strains placed on all families by poverty and unequal access to education.

Only once during the hour did Rev. Furrer's face get anywhere near a smile. In fact, he looked downright grim. He even noted, after mild applause for the Sondheim singers, that he's "not much for clapping in worship service, but it's hard not to." Low joy quotient in this church, I ruled, in spite of the Sondheim. Why stand on such expressive solemnity if your theology is so loose? On the other hand, the retired ladies at the entryway desk had been very friendly. And even though I passed on the opportunity to introduce myself as a visitor, the church obviously was trying to make newcomers welcome.

As I had pulled up to the Unitarian Universalist church that Sunday morning, I saw a man walking the labyrinth that had been created in the church yard. I'd never walked one myself but had heard that many people find it to be a meaningful spiritual exercise. Maybe that was the UU lesson for me: Even though a particular spiritual path may look uninviting to me, others might find that it leads them on a meaningful journey. And because the UUs didn't seem to be out to convert, conquer, or persecute those who believe other than they do, I couldn't find fault with them.

Looking back on this chapter, I find variations of "judge" and "judges" recurring; in other places, the concept of judgment is implied. I may be wrong about this, but it seems to me that the tenets of this congregation have more to do with love and acceptance than with judgment—something that is probably better left to the divine than to us struggling humans who are searching for and striving to emulate the divine.

St. Elias the Prophet
Greek Orthodox Church
June 20, 2004

With its white-washed exterior and cruciform shape thrown into relief by the desert hill behind it, St. Elias the Prophet Greek Orthodox Church is one of the most distinctive Santa Fe County churches. Though it looks as if it had been picked up from a Greek hillside and transplanted in New Mexico, it was built here in 1992. Step inside, and you enter a world thousands of miles and centuries removed from twenty-first-century Santa Fe.

The pure, white, spare exterior is bright but calming. Open a simple blue door and all your senses are assaulted. Eyes flood with saturated color and an abundance of pattern. Nostrils are tickled by incense. Ears echo with reverberant chant.

When you enter the narthex, the sanctuary is straight ahead behind what Orthodox Christians call the iconostasion—a wall of colorful painted figures, or icons, that has three doors. David and I were preoccupied with inconspicuously finding a seat, so we didn't have a lot of straight-on face time with the iconostasion, though we could see a portion of it from the side. The Orthodox Church's Web site says that the figures on the right are always Christ and John the Baptist while the left has depictions of Mary and the church's patron saint. The sanctuary is where the priest and his assistants hang out for most of the service, hidden from view for most of the congregation.

Though not as intricate as the mosaic floors found in Italy's historic churches, St. Elias's floor tiles are highly patterned for a contemporary Christian church. As we passed through the center of the church, the nave, light drew my eyes from the floor to the ceiling. The central dome is painted a deep blue and adorned with a multitude of biblical figures whose identities are spelled out in Greek. More figures are painted on the columns supporting the dome.

Blue, gold, and red predominate. Some of the gold—especially in the painting of the Last Supper that crowns the iconostasion—looked as if it were gilt rather than simply paint. At a lower level along the iconostasion, we could see ornamental flower and ribbon medallions. A few frescoes are painted on other walls, but the crown jewels are clearly the dome and the doors to the sanctuary.

Overall, the quality of artwork is notable, its style clearly deriving from European traditions rather than Santa Fe's Spanish and pueblo architectural and artistic influences.

We received a bulletin from the woman at the door and took seats in folding chairs set up in the north transept, facing a quartet of chanters (including one woman) who were standing at a shared music stand, just as they would have in Renaissance Europe. My first thought was that the folding chairs were rather tacky, considering the room's splendor. After a while, the spartan seating began to make sense.

We took seats, but we didn't sit in them, because everyone else was standing. The back of the bulletin explained "Proper Decorum in an Orthodox Church" to include standing for all but the epistle reading (and, as it turned out, the sermon). Furthermore, when parishioners do sit, because they believe God to be mystically present in the church, they find it "customary and right" to sit without crossing their legs. Hmmm, I thought. I believe God is everywhere, not just in church, so that would mean never crossing my legs. However, I don't recall any biblical passage forbidding such a practice, so I'm not going to give it a second thought after I leave this church.

Let me say right now that the most memorable aspect of the service was the prolonged standing. Of the hour and a half that we were there, we sat only for the sermon, which ran no more than a dozen minutes. On either side of the sermon we stood—even for the epistle. Toward the end of both sessions, I had to sit. This visit turned out to have bad timing for me, as I had had major surgery the previous Monday and was still a bit weak and had swollen feet and ankles. I joined the one elderly, infirm woman who sat through the entire service (in fact, she snoozed through a good portion of it).

Though folding chairs were set in rows in the north and south transepts, the walls facing the sanctuary were lined with what appeared to be overgrown choir seats—tall, wooden stalls with narrow, flip-down seats and high armrests. Those in the know, I decided, chose the stalls so they could help support themselves by their forearms when standing.

As we arrived, just before ten o'clock, the sun shone through the dome's eastern deep-set window, and the resulting angled pillar of light was given dimension by incense hanging in the air. It reminded me of the Pantheon's oculus.

Even though we were a few minutes early, the service seemed to have started; the singers kept on chanting their modal, largely monophonic tunes in three octaves well past what we'd think of as prelude time. There was no instrument of any kind, but the space was well designed for unaccompanied chant and reverberated with its low tones throughout the service. If you were a soprano, your voice really stood out. Mine wasn't one of those voices, because we had access to neither words nor music.

The vast majority of the service was chanted rather than spoken, and it might as well have been Greek for all we understood. Yes, it really was Greek, and it really was incomprehensible. All except for "Amen," which they pronounced "Ah-MEEN." Notable exceptions in English were the Lord's Prayer, the Nicene Creed, the epistle, and the gospel reading.

The constant chanting, sometimes including the congregation, set up a low buzz undergirding worship. At a couple of points in the service the priest, who was usually hidden from us by the iconostasion, spoke words we couldn't clearly make out while the chanters sang above his prayers. Add a layer of bells on the swinging incense burner and you got a sound texture as Byzantine as the artwork.

When the Very Reverend Father Seraphim Poulos finally appeared in the nave, he confirmed every preconception of what an Orthodox priest looks like: full beard, glasses, ornate red brocade vestment over an embroidered white underrobe plus, during some portions of the service, a black hat with veil. His four male assistants, one a young boy, also were bedecked in brocade and carried lamps on long poles.

Aside from the woman in the chant choir, the only other woman participating in the service read the epistle. As she stood in the nave to read, her five-year-old son clung to her legs and made quite a spectacle of himself, which she blithely ignored, all of which I took to be a sign that Greek boys are overindulged.

It was Father's Day, and though Father Poulos noted that it was not a church holiday, he acknowledged that it is a holiday celebrated in this country, so he preached on God as Father. He started by noting that naming God as Father doesn't mean God isn't also Mother and that all our human words for God fall short of God's reality. However, he ended up defending the Father title by virtue of that fact that God had a Son, which makes him always Father. Whereas there wasn't anything in his sermon that we found particularly objectionable, it also wasn't an inspiring or thought-provoking sermon. This may be an overgeneralization, but when you've got a religious tradition that values the past above all else, in which there's nothing new under God's sun, I can't imagine that sermons are very original or meaningful. I wonder if Father Poulos ever relates his sermons and the readings to the daily lives of his parishioners. There was little of that the Sunday we heard him.

The prayers that we heard and understood in English did include a petition "for all mankind" but, with the exception of prayers for the repose of a man's soul, we heard no personal petitions, which again contributed to the sense that worship is essentially rote.

After the sermon, I heard English words that are associated with the Great Thanksgiving, which leads up to Holy Communion, but, like the opening liturgy, St. Elias's communion liturgy was the longest on record in my experience. At one point bells in the bell tower rang, and I realized how few churches have or use bells anymore.

We got a second mini-sermon just before the Orthodox were welcomed to communion. Father Poulos set up this lesson in the context of reminding his parishioners of church doctrine so that they couldn't say, after he left (in a couple of weeks) that nobody had ever taught them the meaning of Holy Communion. His primary message was that those who had not forgiven everyone in their lives should not approach the chalice. If they did, they were warned that the holy wine would burn their throats like a "hot coal." When I hear such "special lessons" from clergy, I can't help wonder if there's a subtext, because there usually is. What were the circumstances of this priest's departure? Was he leaving voluntarily? Had the cause of his departure created a schism in the congregation?

There's a wonderful hymn by Marty Haugen titled "All Are Welcome." It certainly could never be sung at St. Elias. This was the first church (other than the Missouri Lutheran Church in which my husband grew up) that expressly forbid those not baptized and confirmed in its faith to receive Holy Communion. We were asked not to approach the Holy Chalice but were told we were allowed to receive the holy bread distributed at the end of the service. What sophistry, I thought, must be required to justify sharing bread but not wine with "outsiders."

Distribution of the elements itself was unique. As communicants approached the priest, who held the chalice, they lifted the red cloth that seemed attached to the chalice and held it under their chin. The priest used a tiny long-handled spoon to scoop drops of wine from the chalice and deposit them in the congregant's mouth. Then those who had received the wine kissed the red cloth and moved on to the next station, where an acolyte held a basket of bread cubes. Members munched on the bread as they returned to their chairs or stalls. Aside from the wine-receiving ritual, the most notable difference in this celebration of the Lord's Supper was switching the order of bread and wine. The cynic in me wondered if that was just another way the Orthodox sought to distinguish themselves from the Roman Catholics. I mean, in every account of the Last Supper, Jesus blesses the bread and gives it first, before the wine, so why would such a self-consciously conservative religious tradition break with that biblical order?

The Eastern Orthodox Church is known as the Greek Orthodox Church because it refers to early Christians who spoke Greek (though not all spoke Greek). But its origins are really only a thousand years old, dating from the Great Schism with the Roman Catholic Church in 1054, according to the denomination's official Web site. It's quite proud of being "conservative" and of being intertwined with the cultural life and traditions of many of the nations where it is prevalent. It considers itself the only one true Catholic church. For all its foibles, the Roman Catholic Church has at least evolved more over the past ten centuries than its Orthodox counterpart.

How would the service we experienced help one feel close to God? I wondered. It wouldn't do anything for me. Perhaps if I were Greek born and bred I'd have some mystical associations with all the gestures and icons. Applying the joy test, neither of us saw more than one woman smile during the entire service. Nor was the music what I'd call joyful to our ears.

Because there was no printed liturgy in the bulletin and very few people even held books, I assume that the worship service doesn't vary much. Would some parishioners even notice if it did? Do all young congregants learn Greek at home so they can understand worship? They'd have to know the language so they'd know when to cross themselves, which happened more than in any other church I had attended. Even the crossing was different than what you'd see in a Roman Catholic Church—an Orthodox cross, I'm sure.

"Truly strange," was David's unsolicited initial comment as we left the church. He meant, in part, that it was like visiting another country. "Until you have an experience like that, you can forget how diverse our population is." Then he complained about the length of the service and the torture by standing. I tried to make him feel better about the time spent with the Byzantines by reminding him that it had been a great opportunity for a choral musician, because a wealth of choral literature evolved from this church—especially the Russian Orthodox tradition.

On the drive home, David was pretty vocal about how unwelcoming the church was and pointed to such evidence as the absence of any signs on the road—or even on the church until you hit the front door. For whatever reason, I figure they're not looking for new members. As long as the ones they have can support the church financially, I guess they don't need to attract non-Greek worshippers who might want to challenge any of the church's traditions—which obviously just isn't done. We felt further excluded when the man passing the money basket clearly ignored my outstretched hand holding a bill.

I respect the right of Orthodox Christians to worship as they see fit, and I'm sure there's something comforting about being in a time-warp to those who have been raised to believe that unchanging tradition alone can provide salvation. However, for anyone inclined to convert, it would take a long time to become accustomed to this church, for custom is all-pervasive and sacrosanct.

St. Elias the Prophet Greek Orthodox Church is the closest church to our home geographically but one of the furthest from our sensibilities and beliefs.

Religious Science Center
of Santa Fe
June 27, 2004

I learned a lot by attending the "Sunday Celebration Service" with the Religious Science folks.

For example, I was exposed to Wavy Gravy for the first time (I'm too young to have experienced Woodstock), who is, I learned from a postchurch Web search, more than a Ben & Jerry's ice cream flavor. I also learned that there's a difference between Religious Science and Scientology—the former founded by Ralph Waldo Emerson lover Dr. Ernest Holmes; the latter by L. Ron Hubbard. (My visit took place a year before Tom Cruise's behavior put Scientology in all the media.) I even got to experience, rather than just read about, a storefront church.

The congregation meets in what must at one time have been a retail store. David and I sat in the back row, which meant that our heads were inches from the vertical blinds covering the plate-glass windows that looked directly out on the sidewalk. The front of the worship space had been renovated to create a stage with plastered and tiled walls and recessed lighting. Deep purple meeting room chairs were arranged in a horseshoe on purple carpeting. Although the minister noted that the woman providing the day's special music was also creating a stained glass piece for the front doors, the sanctuary bore no "religious" decoration of any sort.

What looked as if it could be a large, glass-walled cry room for young children turned out to be a "toxic-free partition" for members with environmental sensitivity. There was even a request in the bulletin that attendees "consider coming to Church scent-free" in consideration of those who are sensitive to scents.

We arrived just as the service was starting with the prelude—a quiet, drifty, meditative-like improvisation on piano. Then the Reverend Bernardo Monserrat led a reading of their call to worship: "There is a power greater than we are and we come this morning to learn how to use it and to learn how to have it use us. By remembering God and reminding each other we know peace."

The meditation song that followed repeated these ideas: "I am loved . . . I am strong . . . I am whole . . . The All of God is in my life." Whoever wrote the words and music (to which we weren't given access) was a mystery. The melody of the second congregational song was vaguely familiar; its text was about letting go and letting the Spirit guide one's life. After singing the two verses a first time, the minister added some rhythm with a hand drum that he had slung over his left shoulder, and the woman who had read the day's texts—an RSC licensed practitioner (whatever that is)—shook maracas while the congregation swayed and bopped through a couple more repetitions.

As the offering was being collected, everyone sang an Alleluia, and after placing their offering in the basket, each person stood, joined hands with a neighbor, and started swaying and singing. We remained standing for the closing Peace Song: "Let there be peace on earth" with slightly modified text. Two preschoolers and their attendants joined the congregation at this point as each row of worshippers swayed. The shifting of balance was not, however, *to* the music, which made me want to go up on the stage and direct their movement. The experience was reminiscent of watching Lutherans try to sway to black gospel music.

It must be a challenge for new religions to develop a hymnody, a corporate song to encapsulate beliefs and to set the mood for various portions of their services. For one thing, those that, like Religious Science, set out to break with the past don't have tradition to build upon. They don't have a hymn book that represents a repository of older and newer songs that those of their belief can share across geography.

The Sunday we visited, a member named Skye had written a composition for piano, voice, and flute that she called "Prayer Song." Her text was clearly Religious Science in theology and spoke of her mind creating her reality. Though David deemed it not terribly sophisticated musically, it was a better-than-average home-grown composition, and the congregation gave her a standing ovation. Would it one day find a place in a Religious Science songbook?

The musical poverty of such new traditions bothers me. Singing can give us access to a spiritual realm, and church is about the only place where most people have a chance to sing and to experience corporate song, which is why the music should be something worthwhile. That's not to say that there aren't mainline Christian churches whose musical offerings aren't just as nutritionally poor, both spiritually and musically.

An absence of a long and strong tradition was evident in the readings and sermon, aka "lecture," as well. What was billed in the bulletin as "Spiritual Mind Treatment" turned out to be two readings: one from *Practical Spirituality* and the other from Wavy Gravy's *Something Good for a Change*. These were followed by prayers. Several individual petitions were offered. Each ended first with the petitioner and then the congregation saying, "And so it is" (which goes by "Amen" in Christian denominations). If that was the "science of mind" treatment, it was lost on me. The science part, I mean. In fact, there was no moment in the service in which the scientific principles of this faith were apparent. If anything, the church's principles were of the social science kind, and their proofs were anecdotal rather than quantitative.

Rev. Monserrat's lecture theme was "If I were God, how would I be?" After taking answers from the congregation, he worked around to saying that the God in us is, or can be, all the attributes they had just assigned to God: loving, peaceful, busy, fun. . . . He made multiple references to "God's presence in you," emphasizing that Religious Science believes not in a God that's "out there" and who must be appeased but in a God that is present in every living thing, including all people. I can see how the emphasis on the universal mind or consciousness and the oneness of all the universe would be appealing to those feeling disconnected from the divine and who long for world peace.

Though the lecture was moderately interesting, at least in its novelty, I found myself wondering afterward how different the message could be from one service to the next. From what I could tell, Religious Science observes no liturgical year, celebrates no religious festivals, and practices no communal rituals or sacraments. Those may all have been dismissed as remnants of old ways of thinking that don't sustain these believers. However, I believe there's still a part of the primal human in us that yearns for ritual, for marking the seasons, for reenacting the cycle of birth, life, and death in some way. I would miss a larger context for worship if I became a regular in this congregation. I might also miss the oft-retold, multicharacter stories that you get in the Judeo-Christian tradition. Stories of a founder born less than a century ago can only be stretched so far.

Another strain of Religious Science belief (or so I gathered from my one-hour exposure to it) is the power of positive thinking and of the mind's ability to influence the circumstances of one's life. Whether or not you believe that is so, what have you got to lose? It seems entirely plausible to me that, by focusing on good outcomes and looking for the good, love, and beauty in any situation, we would be happier, more peaceful and content, even if all our intended outcomes didn't materialize. And though there was a lot of focus on self-affirmation and self-development throughout the service, Rev. Monserrat also pointed out that acknowledging the God in you means not just doing what you want but what God wants—what's good for others and the world.

I can see how some might argue that there's an overemphasis on self-realization in churches like Religious Science and Unity. That may be true, but it's also true that not everyone is at the same point on their spiritual path, and not all who consciously seek a rich spiritual life find guidance in the same places. For some people, long-established religions and denominations overemphasize human shortcomings and assert their particular religious practice as the only hope for redemption with such aggressiveness that those individuals can simply fall into despair—despite any countervailing message of God's love and grace. The messages that members of such churches may internalize goes something like this: I am not worthy of divine love, and I need the church's sanctioned leaders to absolve me because I'm not encouraged to seek grace directly in a relationship with God or through Christ's life and teachings or through the inspirational intervention of the Holy Spirit.

Reformation shouldn't be a once-in-recorded-history movement.

One thing I appreciate about some of the newer religions is the recognition that spirituality is broader and deeper than what we can access via traditional religious texts—the Bible or Torah or Koran. Whereas the "early Church Fathers" and many of their counterparts today were, and are, concerned about limiting the number of texts deemed to be divine revelation, some of the newer religions see the potential for spiritual truth in more diverse, even offbeat texts, like Wavy Gravy's *Something Good for a Change*. No matter how you look at them, the traditional religious texts come from an era far removed in time and space from our daily lives. Though many of their foundational truths may be as valid today as when they were written, their stories—including their moral codes—were inevitably framed by a historical context that can seem emotionally inaccessible and practically absurd to today's worshippers.

Roughly a hundred and fifty people attended the Religious Science service on the Sunday we visited. At least ten were visitors. And though we didn't draw attention to ourselves as guests, those who did were welcomed, offered a flower, and told of information about the church that was available in the entryway. It seemed a friendly congregation in other ways as well. During the welcome time, there were plenty of smiles, greetings, and hugs. One announcement concerned an upcoming congregational picnic at a member's house. After the service, a woman who had sat a few chairs down from us, introduced herself and explained that she'd been a member for twenty years and said, "This is a good place to be." We beat Rev. Monserrat out the front door, and though he didn't try to corral us, he did say, "Thanks for coming!" After the Orthodox Christians the week before, here was a truly warm and inviting community.

The fact that religions like Unity and Religious Science exist and are popular (at least in some areas of the country) points out the need that people feel for a faith and a worship experience that affirms their goodness, not just their shortcomings, and that reminds them that if God is present in all of creation (as the Bible says), then God is also in them. That recognition of the connection between human and divine is more than just a palliative for the human condition. It can be an inspiration for "divine intervention" in daily life. Those who pray the Lord's Prayer (though we did not with the Religious Scientists) say, "Thy will be done on earth as it is in heaven." If we are to be instruments of God's will, then remembering that God is within us, we may be led to act in more godly ways out of love rather than out of fear. After all, it was Jesus who said that, of faith, hope, and love, the greatest is love.

THE RELIGION PAGE

If coverage of religion in the local newspaper is any indication of the value a community assigns to its spiritual life, then Santa Fe qualifies as a very spiritual place. Every Saturday, two full pages of *The Santa Fe New Mexican* are devoted to listings of services and events sponsored by religious and other spiritual organizations. However, on the Saturday before Holy Week 2004, three whole pages listed services and other events—and that didn't cover every offering; readers were directed to the paper's Web site for a full listing.

Some weeks the religion page simply presents a directory of faith communities, organized by denomination or, in the case of non-Christian groups, by other defining characteristics. The first week of April, these other subheads included: Course in Miracles, Prophetic, Self-Realization Fellowship, and New Thought (under which heading fell "The Celebration," "Church of the Creative Spirit," "Spirit Heart Sanctuary," "Spiritual Renaissance Center," "Sunrise Community Church," "Symphony of Love," and "Santa Fe Center of Universal Truth for Better Living").

To sample the services of even one group from each category would take far more than the time I'd allotted to my church-touring project.

And then there were all the extra-worship activities. I'd attended the interfaith discussion of Mel Gibson's *The Passion of the Christ,* but that was just one event in a catalog of intriguing seminars, retreats, and spiritual experiences.

In March, yard work deadlines loomed, so I passed up the Faith Alliance Festival, an interfaith arts festival that one participant dubbed an "ecumenical Woodstock." On Wednesdays in Lent the Santa Fe Center for Universal Truth offered "a program for accelerated spiritual growth" (which sounded like the equivalent of a course in speed reading) while Holy Faith Episcopal Church offered musical meditations. Meditation for all faiths could be practiced with a yoga group. Others were invited to find God through dance. Local monasteries held retreats. Catholics and catholic believers of many stripes made the Good Friday pilgrimage to El Santuario de Chimayó. How could anyone with even the slightest interest in things religious or spiritual read *The New Mexican* religion page and not be tempted to partake of the smorgasbord—even if one were a lifelong Lutheran?

Sometimes listings were incorrect. In September, when I called the two listed phone numbers for Islamic communities in order to discover their meeting times, the phone company's computer told me that my calls could not be completed as dialed. Especially given current events, I had wanted to visit with the Islamists, but because I was undertaking this project as a casual visitor, I wasn't going to play investigative reporter just to unearth a correct phone number.

Other times the listings may have been inadvertently misleading, as we discovered the second Sunday in July, when we'd planned to attend the "New Thought" Church of the Creative Spirit. What writer could resist a church with that name?

The paper said the congregation met the second and fourth Sundays of the month. Time, address, and phone number were also supplied. We showed up at ten before the appointed hour at a small office park but saw no sign of other cars or of the Intuitive Healing Center where the creative spirits were to meet. Had they been moved by the creative spirit to gather elsewhere that Sunday? Was news of the new meeting place passed mystically among believers? More likely, we suspected, they'd ceased to meet but had paid for a year's worth of insertions on the religion page. A week later, when I called their number, I was informed by the phone service's automated response system that I'd reached a number that had been disconnected or was no longer in service. It seems the congregants of the creative spirit were no longer in service either.

Reading the religion page presented me with a constant temptation to wander multiple spiritual paths. Every week offered something intriguing, bizarre, or musical. One Saturday in July the paper's listing of the week's religious events included a service at the United Church led by the Santa Fe Men's Camerata; a conversation at the Awakening Museum with a divinity professor and an artist/weaver/mathematician/dreamworker; an icon painting workshop; a healing service at Joyful Ministries; a four-week class on past lives, dreams, and soul travel; and a dozen more options.

Then there were the listings that provided a phone number but no address. In the case of the two Baha'i faith listings that I called in September, one group's number was wrong and the voice mail message for the other Baha'i community asked for the caller's phone number but didn't provide meeting times or place. Highly uninviting. Why should I give my personal information if they won't give theirs? Baha'i dropped off my list permanently.

And then there were those that didn't list on the religion page. For one congregation, I suspect, a listing among the masses didn't provide a sufficiently high profile. In September I first noticed an ad for Christ Church. It was in the Friday *Pasetiempo* arts and entertainment supplement to the newspaper. I'm a sucker for interesting graphic design, and that's what caught my attention. (See my chapter on Christ Church for the full story.)

More than one church shunned the religion page. The morning I drove to Christ Church, I passed a Jehovah's Witnesses church. I'd noticed it before, but that morning it dawned on me that I'd never seen the JWs listed on the religion page. Now, that's either ironic or disingenuous, I thought. Here's the religious group most known for door-to-door proselytizing in this country, but they're not making their presence public by publishing their whereabouts in the paper.

A quick Google search turned up a site—an online support group, if you will—for those who have left the Watchtower Society, as JWs' association is known. Like the Catholic Church, it claims that it's the one true religion and the only way to God.

The JWs have much in common with Seventh-Day Adventists, so I didn't feel compelled to sample JW services. In particular, both groups have a history of predicting the "rapture" or Armageddon—the return of Jesus and the end of the world. That unreliable Jesus, though, he just keeps missing the arrival dates they set for him.

In fact, it was a panel discussion on the rapture that seemed to offer as good a stopping point as any for this project (see the penultimate chapter). That, too, was announced on the religion page.

After a year's perusal of the religion page, and considerable time spent sampling the services advertised there, I realized just how emblematic it is of the City Different. In this city—where, historically, Catholicism butted heads with, tried to subsume, and eventually developed a "don't ask, don't tell" détente with the spiritual beliefs of Native Americans—a great multiplicity of beliefs has found fertile ground over the years.

Here, discussions of spirituality are an everyday phenomenon. I'm talking about the chance meetings at Whole Foods supermarket that spark discussions of spiritual matters between shoppers and serendipitous events given spiritual interpretation by customers waiting in an auto repair shop.

I appreciate the paper's nonjudgmental attitude about all the opportunities for spiritual discovery, growth, and conversation. There seems to be a deep respect for the diversity of spiritual practices that have found a home here. It may be one of the rare examples of encouraging civil discourse in this country today.

Eckankar—Religion of the Light and Sound of God
July 18, 2004

I knew I was in for a different sort of service when I entered the small conference room in an office park and saw nothing noteworthy at the front of the room other than a framed photograph of a middle-aged white guy wearing a suit and glasses. Though he looked as if he could be a Midwestern insurance salesman, he had to be the religion's leader, I correctly assumed. As I learned later that morning, the man in the photo, Harold Klemp, runs Eckankar from Minnesota.

Later in the service one of the members explained to me that when you become a member of Eckankar, this pasty-faced guy (though she didn't describe him that way) enters your soul in a manner similar to how Christians might describe the presence of the Holy Spirit and, I think the point was, helps you on your karmic journey.

No, thank you! I said to myself. I'll take a faceless Christian version of the Holy Spirit before some guy who looks like a salesman and claims to be able to show me the way to God.

Of the seventeen people who assembled the morning I visited, one was in his thirties, a couple of us were somewhere in our forties, and the rest wouldn't see fifty again. There were only three couples among the assembly. Two men were by themselves, and the balance were middle-aged and elder women. All were Anglo. No children attended, and after the service I wondered what a child would get out of Eckankar worship.

The EKists, as they call themselves, get high marks for being friendly. Three women seated near me introduced themselves before the service, one gave me a newcomer's information packet, and twice I was invited to sign the guest register so I could receive mailings of their newsletter. I declined the last, explaining that I was visiting a number of churches and didn't want to get on any mailing lists. The woman to my right said that visiting multiple churches sounded interesting. She had recently started attending EK services, and I couldn't help wondering what brought this single, fiftyish woman wearing braces to this group. I nearly made the suggestion that she visit a few more churches before committing to this one.

The absence of instruments was a warning not to elevate my hopes for music, but even my modest expectations were crushed. After a brief explanation of the service by a husband and wife team who were leading worship, the wife read a short passage about "the law of love" from a book written by Klemp. Then we were invited to sing "Hugh," which we were told is an ancient name for God. I learned later that they spell it "HU," but all I could think about, completely inappropriately, was the actor Hugh Grant.

Though everyone else closed their eyes for the God chant, I kept mine open and watched. Some people looked relaxed, but there was no joy in their singing the name of God. The "singing" consisted of a single pitch. It wasn't even a unison pitch, which might have—had it been in perfect tune—created some interesting, consciousness-raising overtones. Nor was the Hughing in harmony. I gave the EKists a failing grade for musical enlightenment.

After about three minutes of the EKists' version of "Om," we had a few moments of silence and then the husband leading the service proclaimed, "Let the blessings be" or "May the blessings be," which I took to be an "Amen" to their opening meditation. The wife introduced the topic of the day's discussion and told a few stories that were designed to demonstrate the law of love and, specifically, that to get love you must give love. I immediately thought of the famous Beatles' lyric on the same theme. What I wouldn't have given to hear that music instead of the haphazardly intoned "HU."

When the leaders asked us to break into three groups to discuss three statements about the law of love, I felt as if I'd wandered into a conference. My group of six women was to discuss how "the law of karma is the law of love in action." Not knowing squat about the EKists' law of karma, I offered to listen. Our group's leader, a woman who could have been just on either side of seventy, tried to make me feel like part of the group by providing brief explanations of the insider terms the others used—like "Mahanta," which I originally heard as "Mahatma." Judging by appearance, our group leader could have been a Midwestern Lutheran grandmother. I recognized her face and her energy. However, the way she talked about dreams and karma and the Mahanta (aka Klemp, whom they call the Living ECK Master) made it clear that appearances can be deceiving.

Four of the women shared personal stories about some karmic episode that manifested the law of love. The woman to my left had been divorced two years earlier after a twenty-seven-year marriage and was about to adopt a boy from Liberia. She told a story that involved her driving from her home in Albuquerque to an EK service in Santa Fe. She turned on her car radio to National Public Radio and hit the Sunday morning gospel program, which David and I have enjoyed when we get a chance to hear it. She wondered if she should turn it off, and I wanted to say, "What?! You're afraid that a little Christian gospel music might contaminate your soul?" But I kept quiet while she explained that, just as she was thinking of tuning out, she saw a billboard with the words "Expect something BIG," so she took the sign as a sign to leave the station on. Shortly thereafter the program host announced that the next song was titled "Going Home to God." Apparently, that's a major catchphrase for EKists, so my neighbor took the announcement as a sign of good karma and turned the radio off. At that point I couldn't keep silent. I had to ask, "Why didn't you listen to the song?" She replied that she'd gotten the message and didn't need to hear any more. Our leader chimed in that maybe someone else would have needed to listen to the words. "You're missing the point!" I wanted to say. "It's about the *music!* If the title jazzes you, the marriage of words and music in a good gospel song has got to lift you even higher." But I wasn't out to convert the EKists to good music, so I held my tongue.

I held it again when the group leader talked about how she still struggled to not judge others. She'd been reading a book about Hitler and decided that some of the goals he had weren't necessarily bad in themselves, and so she decided that even in cases like Hitler's we shouldn't judge others. "Wait just a minute!" I wanted to exclaim. "Don't you think you're being just a little naïve? *You* may be full of love, but we don't yet have a world in which everyone is full of goodness and light. Loving your enemy is fine, but if she comes after your child with a gun, you mean to say you're not going to stop her by any means possible?" And I used to think I was a political liberal.

Aside from the absence of spiritual sustenance via music (completely ironic, in my view, for a church purporting to be about the sound of God) and my suspicion of a religion in which the leader makes himself the pathway to God—both factors that make it highly unlikely that I'd ever convert to EK—the EKists themselves seemed to be nice people truly seeking spiritual development.

And maybe that's where mainstream Christianity has an Achilles heel and where newer alternative religions, whatever their roots, have an advantage. The long-established denominations I'm familiar with don't talk much about personal spiritual growth or encourage self-discovery of God. Their answer to "spiritual growth," if you were to ask about it, would likely be to follow the rubrics of their particular denomination and pray (rather than meditate, which would seem too self-centered).

Despite the focus on the law of love when I visited, all is not goodness and light. EKists believe in karma and reincarnation, so they're motivated to act in what they see as kind and loving ways. Whether it's the threat of hell or the fear of a nasty reincarnation, most religions seem to have a stick lurking behind the front door even if they hang a carrot by the doorbell.

When I got home and glanced through the materials I'd been given, they explained that the light and sound of God in the religion's name refers to the Holy Spirit, known to EKists as the ECK. As the EK brochure points out, Moses and Saul (later Paul) are just two who experienced the light of God. Their explanation of the "Sound of God" was even less convincing and was explained as the wind the disciples heard at Pentecost as well as the sound of water, of creatures in nature, or of musical instruments. So where *were* those musical instruments in EK worship?

Among the other EKist beliefs that I'd gotten an inkling of during the service was their belief in a "spiritual eye" between your eyebrows, which I recognized immediately as corresponding with the "third eye" or sixth chakra or energy center recognized in various Eastern beliefs. Certain traditions originating in the East also share with Eckankar a belief in the existence of several physical and spiritual planes of existence.

According to the literature I was given, those who become members must spend at least two years studying ECK before they may seek "initiation" in ECK. On the one hand, this might sound a bit cultish to some, but Christian traditions have similar requirements for initiation into church membership by "confirmation" or "first communion."

After writing a first draft of this chapter on the afternoon of my visit with the EKists, I felt the need to purify my ears and soul, so I sat down at my piano and sight-read through some Bach. I hadn't touched the piano since Christmas, but I felt the need to hear some inspired sounds. I randomly chose a five-part fugue in five flats from Part I of *The Well-Tempered Clavier.* Bach doesn't make sight-reading easy, and my playing wasn't concert hall quality—especially given my long hiatus from the keyboard—but even stumbling through J.S. Bach's fundamentally awesome, musically sophisticated composition gave me hope that human sounds other than "Hugh" can contain echoes of and glimpses of the divine even when they're not overtly religious.

CHURCH OF CHRIST
AUGUST 1, 2004

In a prayer offered at the Church of Christ on Galisteo Street in Santa Fe, the prayer leader proclaimed that this congregation was seeking to be one of "simple Christians." Ah, such an honorable goal—so fraught in its execution with issues of interpretation and politics. Even the congregation's tradition of shape-note hymn singing turned out to be less simple than it seemed.

At least the building is simple, consisting of an unremarkable pueblo-style shell. Inside, industrial blue carpet, white walls with a lavender paint "wainscoting," no banners, and no cross. At odds with the spareness of décor was the white lace–trimmed empty bulletin board in the narthex—the first thing I saw as we entered. An elderly ladies auxiliary had been at work. It appeared that the ladies auxiliary had also been in charge of window coverings, which consisted of neutral-colored blinds dressed with a flounce and valance of royal blue. The sanctuary smelled musty—unexpected in dry Santa Fe.

Rose seat pads softened the pews, which were slightly banked toward the front of the church, where two shorter pews flanked the chancel. Before the lectern, placed front and center, was a tourist-grade Southwest-style vase filled with artificial flowers. Behind the lectern in the lavender-painted chancel was a keyhole recessed area that I'm guessing held the church's immersion baptismal fount. A mural had been painted on the back wall behind the font. Rather than depicting a scene from the life of Christ, it showed an adobe structure set in desert scrub, backed by hills, next to a small river in the foreground.

By the time the service started, we—or, rather, David—had been greeted by three men, one of whom turned out to be the minister, Kent Hayhurst. With his short-sleeved maroon shirt and tie, he didn't stand out as being the minister.

The first thing David does when he enters an unfamiliar church is to open its hymnal. And, praise God, this church had one. Just when I was beginning to think that there'd been a hymnal book-burning in Santa Fe, we found a collection of more than a thousand songs that ranged from spirituals to a truncated version of Handel's "Halleluiah Chorus." Many were newer songs written, it seemed, for the Church of Christ.

But the number of selections wasn't what distinguished this hymnal. For the first time in our lives, we held a shape-note hymnal! If you don't know what that is, you won't understand why I pulled out the exclamation point. Shape-note hymnody, also called fasola, has been around the United States since Colonial times but is most closely associated with southern Appalachia. It's an alternate musical notation system in which notes have one of four shapes: triangle, oval, square, or diamond. For people like us who have spent our entire lives reading conventional notation, the shapes were rather distracting.

If you enjoyed the sound track to the movie *Cold Mountain,* you've heard shape-note hymnody. The tradition is also called Sacred Harp singing, after the 1844 hymnal by that name. Even before the movie introduced millions to the Sacred Harp tradition, a resurgence of interest had been building around the country, with fans traveling to weekend singing conventions. It turns out that even Albuquerque has a Sacred Harp singing group that gathers twice a month at, of all places, the Friends Meeting House.

Though this church got high marks for having a hymnal, it had no instruments. All singing was a capella, which, I later learned from the church's Web site, is a theological decision in Churches of Christ. It seems this church believes there's no evidence that early Christians used instruments, so it shuns them today. To the congregation's cred-it, they sang strongly and surely in four-part harmony with only the leadership of a twenty-something young man who stood at the lectern's microphone to lead the singing with his voice and some-times his right hand. Though he was tall and hefty, he slouched, as if uncomfortable with his size or with being on stage, yet his start-ing of the tunes was sure. Sacred Harp harmonization emphasizes fifth and sixth intervals, which gives the music an "open," perhaps primitive sound but also makes it easily singable.

The first selection made me apprehensive about the rest of the service. It was the "Battle Hymn of the Republic." Oh, no, I thought. We're going to have to endure a "God and nation" tirade against all things "liberal." I grew more concerned when the second hymn, a more recent composition, was called "The Battle Belongs to the Lord." However, our politics were spared from attack by the ser-mon, which took as its theme the battle with doubt. Among the postsermon hymns was one of the most familiar Sacred Harp songs to Lutherans: "Come Thou Fount of Every Blessing." Hearing it a cappella in four parts confirmed my conviction that, much as I love organ-led singing, an unaccompanied verse now and then can be powerful. Of course, it's only powerful if the congregation puts its heart, soul, and vocal cords firmly behind the notes.

Though we'd picked up a bulletin, it didn't contain an order of service. Hymn numbers were called out by the song leader. Prayers were spoken by prayer leaders. There was no formal liturgy, though there was a framing prayer before distribution of the bread and before passing of the wine—neither of which we took.

Though I'd taken communion in Missouri Lutheran and Catholic churches—where I wouldn't necessarily have been welcome to do so—at the Church of Christ I passed the plate when I saw what it contained. Actually, I'm still not sure exactly what it carried. Instead of flat white wafers of unleavened bread or bits of grocery store yeasted bread, the plate held small, tan chunks that looked like pellets you might feed a domesticated animal. When David asked if I was going to take communion, I took his query as a plea for a pass on the unidentified morsels and shook my head no.

The sermon preceding the Lord's Supper was passable but not memorable. I was grateful it wasn't delivered in bold and italics. The minister stood behind the lectern, looked at his notes occasionally, and rested his words securely on the lesson of the day from Luke, which recounted the episode in which the imprisoned John sends two of his disciples to ask Jesus if he is the one they'd been waiting for. (Hence the sermon's theme of doubt.) Jesus, ever the indirect interlocutor, tells the messengers to give John a report about all the healing miracles he's been performing.

The most unusual aspect of Rev. Hayhurst's delivery was that he kept his left hand in his pants pocket most of the time. During the prayers and communion at the end of the service, when the leader of the companion Spanish congregation joined the English song leader at the front of the church, I noticed that these two men also keep their left hands in their pockets. I started to wonder if there was some theological significance to their hidden "sinister" appendage.

The relationship between the English- and Spanish-speaking congregants was unique in our experience. As we entered the church we had noticed a door at the opposite end of the building with "Church of Christ" inscribed in Spanish above it. It seems that the Spanish speakers—about twenty-five of them, including a half dozen young children—worship in Spanish by themselves up to the sermon. After the sermon, they join the English congregation for prayers—spoken phrase by phrase first in English, then in Spanish—and communion. It seemed a friendly way to enable worship in everyone's first language while recognizing that all are part of the body of Christ.

In the end, I was grateful that we didn't hear any tirades against feminism from this pulpit. That's not to say that this was a welcoming church for me as a woman. As David pointed out, in the long list of worship and church life assistants for the week, only one woman was listed out of fourteen positions, and she was the hall monitor—whatever that might be. The welcome and announcements, songs, Bible readings, prayers, communion, and outside monitor posts were all held by men or boys. These simple Christians harkening back to the origins of Christianity clearly weren't interested in the historical record that shows women as well as men being active as teachers and healers in the early church.

In some respects, though, the congregation did seem to be remembering the early Christian mission. For example, congregants live their faith by feeding the homeless on the first Sunday of every month. In addition to having a missionary, the Church of Christ practices what I call billboard evangelism. The week we visited, the church's street corner sign bore this message: You can give without loving, but you can't love without giving.

The Churches of Christ Web site proclaims that its churches are nondenominational and have no administrative headquarters or head of the church. They say they seek the unity of all who believe in Christ. They practice no infant baptism; they baptize by immersion those who are old enough to understand what they're doing. They have no creed other than the New Testament and see themselves as having returned to a primitive or original Christianity.

I've always been ambivalent about creeds, so dispensing with one seems fine to me, though somehow or other almost every organization resorts to some form of creed or mission statement or vision statement. For the Church of Christ, I suppose the statement of beliefs on their Web site stands in for a creed.

I've recited the Apostles Creed and the Nicene Creed for roughly four decades. Sometimes I've thought about the words more than other times. Never can I recall completely believing every word as written.

And that was before I ran across Bishop John Shelby Spong's *Why Christianity Must Change or Die.* When I began reading it in September, the first chapter—on the difficulty for "thinking people" of believing the words of the Apostles' and Nicene Creeds—was a major ah-ha experience; here was a respected cleric and theologian clearly articulating what I'd known and felt but not put into words.

But I did already know a little about the history of how the creeds came to be, and I'd been taught the party line about the necessity of expressing what's true about Christ in order to prevent falsehoods about Christ from infiltrating the body of the faithful. That's never been a persuasive argument with me. All it signifies with surety is the desire of a cadre of powerful fourth-century men to impose their beliefs and interpretations of Christ's life on those who disagreed with them. So, whereas I believe a lot of what you'll find in Christian creeds, I chafe at the edict that one must recite the creed weekly to prove one's loyalty to what a bunch of dead guys decreed was the one true way to believe in God.

If Christians are serious about living a Christ-like life, about being "simple Christians," they need to be honest about Christian history and look carefully at what Christ's followers said about his words and deeds (though even that is challenging given the time lag between his life and the recording of it). Our churches need the courage to open the doors of tradition to the now well-documented research showing that much of the dogma undergirding those traditions was the politically motivated work of very human men who were more concerned with solidifying their earthly power than with encouraging others to discover the divine.

Most contemporary Christians take comfort in the familiar, in tradition, and even in words (like those of the creeds) selected to pin down a literal meaning of the Christ experience. Christ himself, on the other hand, was anything but a traditionalist or literalist. He challenged authority. His followers were a motley crew. He healed and welcomed a broad array of outcasts. He lived passionately and enjoyed parties but also promoted charity. His teachings—delivered as metaphor, parable, and koan—are notable for their resistance to literal interpretation.

In one sense, any Christian church could be described as the Church of Christ, yet I wonder how many Christian churches Christ would recognize as his.

Our Lady of the Woods, Wicca
August 1, 2004

Fear makes people do stupid things. So said a bumper sticker that I nearly bought a week before visiting the Wicca coven in Los Alamos, which also serves Santa Fe. My sticker sighting was timely, given the history of how witches and alleged witches have been treated. The older I get the more truth I see in that bumper sticker's statement. Nevertheless, the kinder, gentler self I was trying to become hesitated at calling anyone stupid—even if it were true.

The coven didn't list a phone number in the newspaper, but the group's Web site had been updated July 1, so I assumed it was reasonably current. Its calendar said that Lughnassadh would be celebrated at seven p.m. in North Mesa Park in Los Alamos on Sunday, August 1. There was even a link to directions.

Like most people, I've had no known direct contact with witches and know little about what they're like today. Secondhand sources tell me they're focused on connecting with nature, acknowledging the female aspect of the divine, and in doing good. My friend Sharon, who works at a bookstore, says titles on witchcraft are especially popular with adolescent girls and that the books promote self-esteem and respect for all living things.

I can see the appeal of a belief system that celebrates one's connection with the natural world and with the divine presence in nature. Once again, it's *feeling* and *experience* of the divine, of something larger than our individual human selves, that gives such "alternative" religions a decided edge over mainline Christian denominations. The words of institution, dry wafers that stick to the roof of your mouth, and poor wine are paltry simulacra of the real things—of words as deeds, of earthy food and drink.

So as I headed up the mountain to Los Alamos on Sunday night, I was not afraid of the witches. I didn't think I'd be a likely convert, but I was curious and eager to see the members of this coven up close. Would they all look like middle-aged hippies, wearing cotton skirts and long, graying hair? Or would they be a cross section of Santa Fe eccentrics—some visibly wealthy, some spacey, and some calculatingly cool?

I still don't have the answer to that question, because this was a Sunday of dashed expectations. That morning, David and I had planned to visit the United Pentecostal Church. The paper clearly gave its address on Bishop's Lodge Road and its Sunday service time as ten a.m. We found the address, but the name on the building was for a Seventh-Day Adventist Church, and no cars sat in the parking lot. When we looked at the paper again, we saw that both churches listed the same address. Did they share a building, or was the listing wrong? Not wanting to waste the morning's research opportunity, we scoured the religion page for a service that started at ten-thirty and settled on the Church of Christ of Santa Fe.

That night I drove to Los Alamos and followed directions to the park where the Wiccan gathering was scheduled. Except the park didn't exist. Despite what seemed to be detailed instructions, North Mesa Park was nowhere to be found. I saw a deserted picnic area, a deserted fairgrounds and large stables area, and an empty soccer field, but nowhere on the designated road or in its vicinity was there a park, let alone a park with people. I got to the end of the road and backtracked. Still no park. Had the witches convened and spirited the venue away to an invisible realm? I called David, explained my bafflement, and headed home.

As I drove back to Santa Fe, I wondered what lesson I was supposed to learn by not connecting with the Wiccan community.

Driving into Los Alamos, I was struck by how attractive its setting is. The recent rains had brought to the Jemez Mountains as much green as you ever see in the high desert. In the cloud-filtered light of early evening the black stubble of burned trees blended into the shadowed hillsides, and I wished I'd been able to see the mountain backdrop of this odd city before the Cerro Grande fire of 2000 killed so many trees and destroyed homes abutting the mountains.

Driving back down "the Hill," as the formerly secret mesa is called, I hugged the narrow road around tight curves and made only the briefest glances at the fingers of mesas to my left. Volcanic rock, weather, and time have created a spectacle that may not be as grand as Arizona's famous canyon, yet it is impressive on a smaller scale. Ahead of me sat the waves of the Pecos mountains, and though they'd never replace the Colorado Rockies in my heart, I was grateful to be surrounded by their arms.

The next morning I decided that I did not need organized nature worship in the form of Wicca or any other belief *system*. Every time I take a hike or a walk around the neighborhood I marvel at how the divine expresses itself in the natural world, and I understand that I am a very small and temporal part of a larger living system. Every time I bite into a ripe apricot I send a little prayer of thanks to its creator. Nor do I have to enact prescribed rituals to acknowledge the circuit of the seasons. My body is fully aware of solar cycles and rebels when the days shorten, forcing me to wake in the dark. When we go for hikes, we often take hard-boiled eggs for a mid-morning snack. Eating an egg while sitting on a rock and taking in a panoramic view seems as symbolic a gesture as burning a loaf of bread or anything else the Wiccans might do on Lughnassadh.

SEVENTH-DAY ADVENTIST CHURCH
AUGUST 28, 2004

This is a true story. One hundred and twenty years ago, in a place called Virginia, a group of people wanted to build a church in a town, and they had found the perfect spot. They asked the man who owned the property if they could buy the land next to his house, but he said, "No, I don't like you people, and I don't want your church here." So the people built their church on another empty lot in the town.

About a year after the church had been built, the town experienced a heavy rain and much flooding. In fact, there was so much flooding that the church started floating away from its lot. As the church floated down the road, members tried to steer it with ropes to prevent it from hitting other buildings. But when the church reached a corner, the people couldn't hold the building back, and it turned onto First Street. Then it took a left—despite the members' attempts with the ropes—and settled itself on the lot where the congregation had originally wanted to build. The next day, when the waters receded, the man next door hurried over to the church and gave its members a deed to the property.

That's the story, in paraphrase, that Solomon told during the children's sermon at the Santa Fe Seventh-Day Adventist Church on Saturday, August 28. I lead with that story because the children's sermon was more memorable than the adult sermon and because the power of stories is often greater than the power of sermonizing.

Let me jump right to the sermon proper. "Jump" is a good word for it. A sixteen-year-old boy I'll call William, with dark ear-length hair and long sideburns, dressed in suit and tie, jumped from one

Bible reading to another with scarcely a thread connecting them. Now, I'm willing to grant him generous latitude considering his age, but some other factors made me judge him more rigorously. He noted, for example, that his other sermons had been shorter (this one ran half an hour), so I knew this wasn't the first time he'd been on pulpit duty. He told us that what we were hearing was his fourth draft of the sermon, so, as a former writing teacher, I expected the fourth version to have some merits worth recording. And then there was his attitude. Though he stammered a bit because he'd been working on his sermon rather than sleeping the night before, his predominant demeanor was self-confidence with a few ounces of preacherly swagger and pulpit drifting thrown in. If he wasn't a preacher wannabe, I don't know who is.

Gary Fordham, listed as pastor in the bulletin, didn't seem to be present the day I visited, so I can't tell if William was emulating him or not. I just hope that somewhere along the way to his own congregation the young man encounters someone who can help him shape his homilies a bit more tightly.

He began by reporting on his recent experience at some sort of Adventist youth gathering in Cincinnati. Then he announced that his sermon was on the topic of making choices. Now that's a fine sermon topic and one rich with biblical resources. What he chose were primarily passages presenting law—the Ten Commandments, various Pauline injunctions from the New Testament, one that I think he called "the armor of Christ," and a passage from Proverbs, as I recall. He missed the biggie, though—the one I think of as Jesus' prime directive: You shall love your neighbor as yourself. Taken locally and globally, that's a doozy that few people and fewer nations observe.

I think what William was trying to convey was that, although God gave us free will, he also gave us guidance in the Bible regarding how best to exercise that free will. What mainly came across was that the chosen readings were among his favorites. He would mention a book, chapter, and verse so that those in the pews could look up the passage in their Bibles. Then he'd ask how many had studied that verse and chide or cajole those unacquainted with it. He would read the verse—rapidly, as if racing to the end to show how familiar he was with it. Then he'd offer a few words about how great the passage was. A couple of times he self-deprecatingly noted that his commentary was thin because "I'm not that smart."

The piling on of reading after reading reminded me of the sermon substitute at the Christian Science church. At least in William's presentation, I could tell that these actually were favorite verses that had some personal resonance with him even if he wasn't fully able to communicate their essence to those in the pews.

I believe that one of the main reasons Jesus' life is so powerful and memorable is because of his stories—both the stories he told and the stories about his life. The Jewish Bible, too, is full of stories as well as history and poetry, but it's the narrative element that most sticks in readers' and hearer's minds. The best stories don't yield all their riches on first reading or at least not on first reflection. If they did, both preachers and literary critics would be out of work.

Given the preacher of the day I can't say I had a taste of the typical Adventist service, though in other respects I probably did.

One of the first words I heard after entering the sanctuary was "Satan"—a name rarely heard in other Christian churches these days. It was followed a few minutes later by "the evil one." These references were made in the closing minutes of the preservice Bible study, which I heard after being greeted by two members in the narthex. The woman leading the Bible study closed with a prayer that included a petition asking God to keep the evil one far from their church that day. I wondered if it was a standard request or if the church had experienced some vandalism recently.

It was actually refreshing to hear Satan mentioned. I've never been one to personify evil as Satan, but I've never doubted that evil exists and that fighting evil with truth and love is required of those who believe in God or any kind of divine power or spiritual reality. Nevertheless, I understand the value of personifying evil as Satan just as many people personify the divine as God the Father or God the Son. God the Holy Spirit on the other hand is a bit more wispy, but to me, more powerful.

In terms of wine, women, and song, the Adventists get a mixed rating. The table in front of the pulpit bore the inscription "This do in remembrance of me." Though the Lord's Supper wasn't served the day I visited, I doubted that the Adventists served wine, given their denomination's stance on abstinence from alcohol.

Women certainly were visible and active in leading worship. Though the denomination may be fundamentalist in some respects, it doesn't seem to treat women as second-class members of the body of Christ.

Adventists seem to value song—at least enough to have a printed hymnal in the pews. Singing was led by an aged electronic organ, a piano, and a parishioner who stood at the pulpit's microphone. And though the selections were chestnuts, to put it kindly, I would rather hear them than most of what passes for "praise music." We started with "Open My Eyes," which I didn't know, even though it had the ring of a song that would have been a golden oldie had it been part of my musical upbringing. What interested me more was the accompaniment.

A woman playing piano sat facing a woman playing the organ on the opposite side of the church. Piano-organ duets are difficult at the best of times if only because the attack and sustaining of the tone are so different on the two instruments. In this case I saw more land mines in the shape of ritards at the end of each verse and refrain. The accompaniment wasn't fist-clenching, though. I have to give them credit for trying to make the best of their resources, as the organ seemed incapable of pumping out sufficient decibels to lead singing on its own.

After a call to worship consisting of a portion of Psalm 100 that included a reference to "joyful singing," we sang their introit, "Glory Be to the Father," to a tune I'd never played but recognized as an old standard one for the text. I felt as if I were in a church that hadn't changed its worship music for a century. The collection of "tithes and offerings" was followed by the hymn "Oh When Shall I See Jesus." At that point I had the opportunity to share my hymnal with a mother on my left who was holding her young son. Something as simple as sharing a hymnal with another person can make you feel part of a group.

"Special music" of the day consisted of a husband and wife duet on "How Great Thou Art." All lento verses. Their voices were pleasant enough, but the tune is just so geriatric that I can't take it seriously. The text isn't quite as bad and even has that "contemporary praise song" catchword: *awesome.* Though the sentiment of the hymn is one I could connect with, its syntax and diction could use updating. Now, I realize that some songs are powerful and beloved *because* of their age, and there are many that fall into that category for me, but "How Great Thou Art" isn't on my list.

The melody and rhythm of the African American spiritual "Give Me Jesus," which closed the service, were just different enough from the versions I knew to prevent me from fully enjoying it.

The Adventists' music may have been showing its wrinkles, but the membership was a healthy mix of generations. Only a few attendees were retirement age, the majority were middle-aged, but there were many younger families and at least a dozen preschoolers and a handful of adolescents. If the presence of children signifies the health and future of a congregation, this one's got it made.

This isn't a church in which you sit isolated in your pew, sing a few songs, listen quietly to the sermon, maybe shake your neighbor's hand, and then go home. Through the children I had a glimpse of how tight this congregation is and how everyone knows everybody else. I saw wee ones carrying offering baskets who were led down the aisle by adults I knew weren't their parents. The same kids got passed around the church as if it were the most normal thing. Whether it was to give their parents a break or whether they were being shared with relatives, I couldn't tell, but the children were equally sanguine regardless of who was holding or keeping an eye on them. It truly did seem as if this was one large church family.

Another clue to how the congregation fosters community was revealed as I was walking out to my car. Larry, of the husband and wife duet, called out to me as I headed down the front walk. He invited me to stay for their potluck, which they hold every Sabbath after service. I explained that it was already later than I realized and that I had somewhere I needed to be. I'm sure I would have been faced with a lot of unwelcome questions had I sat down to dine with the Adventists. I'd already done my best to remain anonymous by signing a false name in their guest book and omitting any address. But for the members, I thought, the weekly potluck might be a pleasant gathering. It certainly gave members an opportunity to get to know each other.

Using a number of different metrics, this church ranks high in being welcoming. It had two friendly greeters at the door who introduced themselves and gave me a bulletin that contained service information. When I entered the sanctuary toward the end of the adult Bible study, the woman sitting next to me in the back pew offered me her study handout. Nearly half a dozen other parishioners stopped to shake my hand and welcome me. (I was happy not to be asked to stand or introduce myself during announcements.) Music and words for their hymns were printed in a hymnal. I was even invited to lunch.

Despite the Adventists' friendliness, for the rest of the day they had me confused about what day it was. Because I'd gone to church, I thought it was Sunday, which meant I thought that the next day was a work day. It felt like a cruelly short weekend.

I knew nothing about the Adventists before I visited, other than that they worship on Saturday, so after the service, curiosity compelled me to browse their Web site. The official Adventist Web site explains that the church is preparing the world for the second coming of Jesus Christ. Oh dear, I thought, could they be among the people believing in the literal rapture?

Although the congregation didn't celebrate the Lord's Supper the day I was there, the Adventist Web site says that its celebration involves three symbols: bread, wine, and—something I'd never seen included before—foot washing. Most Christians remember and may reenact foot washing on Maundy Thursday during Holy Week, but that's it.

Though most of their twenty-seven beliefs, taken at face value, seem reasonably similar to other Christian denominations' positions, you get an inkling of what makes Adventists different when you read about "the great controversy" between God and Satan and the "Remnant and its mission," which seems to set the Adventists apart as that faithful remnant of believers in the last times who expect to witness the second coming of Christ. (But how do they know Christ is going to choose them? Aren't they being just a bit arrogant in proclaiming themselves the chosen ones? After all, the Jews claimed that title long before the Adventists. And for all we know, Buddhists might be the ones who are given the insight to see, predict, and witness the second coming of Christ.) One sign of the remnant church, they claim, is the gift of prophesy, which was evident in the ministry of Ellen G. White, an important figure in the early history of the Adventists.

As for behavior, there's talk of abstaining from the "unclean foods" identified in the Bible. But wait a minute. I recall Jesus saying that it's not what goes into your mouth that matters but what comes out of it. He himself didn't have much good to say about Jewish dietary laws. Adventists also abstain from alcohol, tobacco, and illicit drugs. I'm with them on the last two, but Jesus' life and miracles are seriously entwined with the fruit of the vine, so abstaining from wine on theological grounds just doesn't make sense for folks who call themselves Christian.

Though Adventists seem conservative in some ways—they do not condone homosexual relationships or practices—they're progressive in others, for example, recognizing the value of birth control, calling for attention to climate change, speaking out against female genital mutilation, and affirming the role of both men and women in the church. I wondered how closely the members' personal beliefs and practices hued to the denominational line. After all, thousands of Catholics disregard some of that church's decrees about what is acceptable behavior.

There was a coda to this church visit.

The following week, while I was working out of town, I had dinner one night with my friend Sharon. In the middle of a story she was telling, she mentioned "the Devil." That's not a name I'm used to hearing her speak.

Sharon is one of the most spiritual people I know, and that orientation seems to have very little to do with the fact that she was raised Catholic but repudiated Catholicism as a young adult. She was born with a reverence for all life and a sense of the spirit that moves through all creation. Never mind that she's not a current churchgoer, she lives one of the most Christian lives around—a life of caring, nurturing, teaching, volunteer service, pursuit of the truth, and looking for the best in people. So when she mentioned the Devil, I knew we were talking about a phenomenon that wasn't easily explained by her hard science training.

It was about her new car. A used car, actually. A white 1999 station wagon. A week before our dinner, she had put out a fire inside her car. She had opened the back door to retrieve something from the back seat and smelled smoke, so she bent over to look under the car. That's when she saw the flames coming from the interior door molding. Without thinking, she used her hand to suffocate the flame. The plastic, she thinks, protected her hand. I call it a minor miracle.

I saw the damage. A dime-size hole in the black plastic shows where the flames appeared. A splotchy pattern of holes in the ceiling fabric just behind the rear passenger side door was burned by the licking flames.

Sharon immediately called the dealership from which she had bought the car, and someone arrived in short order to investigate the cause of the fire. He asked a lot of questions and checked everything out, but he could offer no explanation for the incendiary event. There was no wiring behind the molding, he claimed. The only theory he could advance—that a cigarette butt had been tossed by someone and had flown in through the partially opened *front* window to land at the back of the rear door molding and start the fire—defies the laws of physics, Sharon said, and I agreed.

Sharon has another theory, and this is where the Devil comes in.

Sharon volunteers at the Humane Society Thrift Store every Saturday morning. Her department is books. She sorts donated books by category, sets aside those that are too beat up to put on the shelf or that she knows won't sell, creates a separate pile of volumes she suspects are valuable (which will be examined by an appraiser), and prices and stocks the rest. Bibles don't sell at the Thrift Store, and Sharon has always felt bad about stacking them in bags for recycling or disposal, so she was happy to collect them for a local church when she heard that it was trying to stock its pews with Bibles. The day of the fire, Sharon's car was full of Bibles. Maybe the fire was the Devil trying to destroy the Bibles, she half-joked with me.

Maybe some evil energy was at work. Even though I might say, like Sharon, that it was "the Devil" at work, I tend to think that negative and, yes, even evil energy is dispersed throughout the universe, and attributing all that destructive energy to one anthropomorphized entity lets the rest of us off the hook a little too easily.

So what did it mean? Did Sharon's car spontaneously combust? If so, how? Did she experience this "accident," which cost her six hundred-plus dollars to repair, just so she could tell me the story and I could use it in this chapter? What were we both supposed to learn from the event? Will we both some day achieve enlightenment where now we only see mystery?

Maybe the universe really does manifest the phenomena we're expecting—the ideas and people and experiences our belief system enables us to see. Are organized religions too eager to make scapegoats or sacrificial lambs out of individuals and people who are too "other," in order to preserve their status quo?

Mountain Cloud Zen Center
August 29, 2004

Years ago, when I met my first Buddhist, I thought, "How odd for a non-Asian to be Buddhist." Those were the days when I assumed that one was born into one's religion, much like one inherited curly or straight hair, a bulbous or a pert nose.

That was before I moved to Boulder, Colorado, and Santa Fe, New Mexico—two small Western cities big on Eastern spiritual traditions. Boulder even has a university—Naropa—based on Buddhist principles. These days I'd be surprised if I met a Buddhist in one of those two cities who didn't have European ancestors.

At least in urban areas, to hear Anglos declare themselves Buddhist no longer seems bizarre. In fact, within what we might call intellectual and progressive circles, Buddhism is often seen as more politically correct than Christianity. Buddhists, it is generally assumed, are less likely to insist that they possess the supreme moral—and hence legal and imperial—authority that leads some Christians into all manner of shameful actions.

I still don't get Buddhism, though. Consequently, I had a difficult time settling in to write about this visit.

✦ ✦ ✦

The week we went to sit at the Mountain Cloud Zen Center, a dozen Buddhist listings appeared on the religion page. I chose Mountain Cloud both because I liked its name and because I knew where it was.

I'd expected a sizable turnout, but David and I composed fifty percent of the attendees. Except for David, we were all women of forty to fifty-some years. The center also holds sittings at other times during the week , so we may have missed its largest gathering.

The only man we saw was one dressed in a long black skirt (cotton or hemp, most certainly) who seemed to be affiliated both with the Zen center and a white van bearing the name of an HVAC company. As we walked from our car toward the slightly earth-bermed main building, the skirted guy had welcomed us and asked, "Are you here to sit with Ann and Jenny?"

"Yes," I replied.

"To sit" seems (and is) so much more passive and uninspiring than "to worship" or "to celebrate." And therein lies one of the big divergences between the Judeo-Christian tradition and Buddhism: Whereas J&Cs worship a supreme being and provide sacrifices (mostly monetary), ostensibly to that being, via the institution of the church or temple, Buddhists don't worship so much as they venerate a special human and employ quiet meditation to look within as a means toward enlightenment—full understanding and release from suffering and pain. There's more of a "prove it" practice in the Judeo-Christian tradition, especially in mainstream Christian churches, that seems to require the speaking of words and singing of songs to demonstrate one's beliefs.

Although many forms of Buddhism exist, they all share a belief in nonviolence, lack dogma, tolerate differences, and usually practice meditation. I find all of those qualities valuable both spiritually and socially. Personally, I struggle most with the meditation part. I fault my upbringing and my culture for that weakness, because mediation has never been a practice I've been encouraged to develop facility in.

On the other hand, Buddhism seems so rudderless and enlightenment so elusive and rare.

To summarize the main worship elements I was monitoring: there was no wine; a woman led the ritual; there was no song; no formal offering was taken. But all those criteria proved irrelevant.

✦ ✦ ✦

The Mountain Cloud Zen Center resembles a small church camp, with a few tiny, metal-roofed cabins assembled near the main building. Minimalist landscaping, gravel paths, and wooden way signs blend into the pine and deciduous tree hillside setting. In fact, the main structure is slung so low to the ground and protected by pines that you could easily miss it.

Inside, after removing our shoes, as requested, we looked around the entry space and in at the mediation room, whose doorway was guarded by two Asian-style gargoyles. Centered in the entryway's window hung a fifteen-inch-diameter brass bell. A gong hung beside it on the wall. At the far end of the meditation room, which had raised wooden frame platforms on either side for seating, stood an altar with statues, a small orchid, votive candles, and an incense burner. Judging from the number of square batting-filled mats—called zabutons, I'd later learn—it could accommodate twenty sitters.

Because no one else was in sight, we picked up booklets that looked as if they might have something to do with the community's gatherings and flipped through them as we sat on chairs facing the front door. The pages seemed to contain chants for a series of rituals. There was no music, and the syllables were nonsensical to me, though an English translation was set on the facing page. Before we could get a fix on what we were looking at, Ann walked through the door, wearing short blond hair, a blue T-shirt, and ivory painter's pants.

She welcomed us, said that anywhere from one to seven people usually gathered on Sunday mornings, invited us to grab as many round cushions as we wanted from the pile, and explained—when she learned that this was our first visit to a Zen mediation center—that they sat for twenty-five-minute intervals punctuated by "walking meditations," which could also be used for restroom breaks.

We walked in behind her on the slightly uneven brown-stained concrete floor. Real adobe walls showed small signs of deterioration—a water mark here, a patch of exposed chicken wire there. Ceiling vigas married Zen and New Mexican influences with their addition of Oriental design stamps.

We watched Ann for cues on how to behave. She arranged her cushions, sat cross-legged on them, set a timer in front of her, and removed her glasses. I wasn't going to miss out on anything by removing my glasses. Then Ann struck the inside of a large metal bowl four times with a covered mallet, letting the broad sound waves dissipate each time before the next strike. I enjoyed the paradoxically hollow yet rich reverberations.

Despite lacking an official focus for my meditation, I found the center a peaceful setting for a sitting. Eight double-hung windows were set high into the wall on both long sides of the room, open to views of pine and locust treetops and raised open an inch or two. It was a calm day. The cords of the raised window blinds hung undisturbed.

All was quiet. Other than our framed view of treetops, the only sensory experience was the slightly sweet smell of incense, which tickled my nose and irritated David's enough to summon a sneeze.

Five minutes after we'd seated ourselves, another woman joined us. She too was dressed comfortably and wore polish on her toenails.

At the end of the first sitting interval, Ann quickly struck the inside of the metal bowl twice. She unfolded herself and stood, faced the altar, made a Namaste bow, and then clapped two wooden bars together before beginning to walk slowly around the small room. We followed.

For me the walking meditation was anything but. Ours wasn't a purposeful gait to get somewhere. Nor was it an energizing walk like those we take around our neighborhood. Neither was it meditative for me. Once again, there was nothing to focus on. Practicing Buddhists may know what they're supposed to do with their mind at such a time, but as a visitor, I was clueless. I couldn't even let my mind relax and find something to concentrate on because I was concerned about not bumping into the person in front of me. Though it may run contrary to some Buddhist principle, I longed for corporate ritual action with a sound track. Even a rhythm would have helped. Maybe I should have approached walking meditation as the haphazard queue that forms for communion in mainline Christian churches.

We made maybe six circuits of the room and then resumed our seated positions on the platform. Another twenty-five minutes passed.

I enjoyed the quiet of the place, interrupted only by intermittent bird calls. I tried to figure out what the statues on the altar represented. One was a Buddha; another depicted a man holding a baton or swordlike instrument above his head; the third was a female figure inside a glass box. Across the room in the middle of the seating platform sat a wooden gong fashioned in the shape of an enormous fish head. On our side was another, more conventionally drum-shaped gong or drum. I longed to strike the fish and hear what sound it made. Then it struck me as funny that a fish would be crafted to make sound.

As we rose for the second walking meditation, David and I both took advantage of the break to leave the room and confer. David offered to wait outside if I wanted to stay, but he could sit no longer, he said. His hips hurt from sitting cross-legged so long. My minimal yoga routines had given me greater flexibility, so I couldn't complain, but I didn't want to sit longer either. I hadn't expected enlightenment in my first hour of sitting, but it hadn't delivered much of anything, and I clearly wasn't prepared to make the most of the opportunity, so I agreed it was time to leave.

Sitting was like writing. For an unschooled and unpracticed meditator, sitting at the Mountain Cloud Zen Center was an experience of watching my mind in suspension between focus and floating to the next word or thought.

THE CELEBRATION
SEPTEMBER 26, 2004

When people speak of "New Age" religion, this may be what they have in mind. The Celebration is listed under the New Thought heading on *The New Mexican*'s religion page, but it offers as much old thought as new. It's more of a stew than anything, for it accepts and celebrates all spiritual traditions. As in a stew, you can pick out recognizable bits and pieces—a cup of Christianity here, a dollop of Judaism there, a sprinkling of Hinduism on top—but the overall flavor is difficult to put into words. Also like a homemade stew, it's never exactly the same from one time to the next, which is to say that the worship service, though structured, is informal and has ample room for variation.

I attended a Celebration service when I did because the newspaper announced that Christine Warren was going to be a guest speaker on "Navigating Change Spiritually: Integrating Endings, Initiating Beginnings." Though I hadn't heard of Warren (who turned out to be a Kripalu yoga teacher and executive coach specializing in change issues), the topic seemed pertinent to the multiple, ongoing changes in my life, so I took the notice as a sign that this was the week to join the Celebrationists.

The group met in a studio at the National Dance Institute. On this Sunday about sixty people had gathered to sit in a semicircle of blue-padded conference chairs in a room with wooden floor, clerestory windows on three sides, and ballet barres on the walls. Against the far wall hung a painted fabric banner with the group's logo: a circle containing images of men and women, religious symbols from many traditions, pueblo dwellings, butterflies, waves, clouds, flames, hearts, and New Mexican mesas. Around the circle were the words of the Celebration's invocation: "We join together to celebrate the splendor of God's love—cherishing all life, honoring all paths, rejoicing in the sacred dance of All That Is. Living in the power of all-embracing love, we affirm our community and acknowledge the divine nature of our humanity."

I was greeted by a man who handed me a bulletin and a blue binder full of song lyrics. As I entered, the musicians were playing gathering music, including "What a Wonderful World." After the striking of a gong we all sang David Pomeranz's "It's in Every One of Us." The instruments included a piano, synthesizer, two guitars, a drum kit, and a bongo. And the players could rock! More important, their faces showed that they were having a good time. At the end of the service I heard someone remark that the drummer was new, but you'd never have known it.

Greetings followed, with several people introducing themselves by their first names and shaking hands. They seemed genuinely friendly, and didn't prod for more information than my name.

Following a welcome from Tracey, the day's host, we stood to sing Chet Powers's "Let's Get Together." The room was full of baby boomers, with the exception of one thirty-something couple holding a toddler and one other woman in her late thirties, also with a toddler. Nearly everyone was moving to the music in their own way. I felt as if I were at a mini Woodstock reunion. Everyone seemed happy and smiled as they sang. The Celebration lived up to its name. In that service, I sensed real joy—a mood, emotion, and energy that's seldom so clearly and widely sensed in other congregations.

The binder collected words but no music for a smorgasbord of feel-good songs from "The Lord's Prayer" and "Amazing Grace" to "On Eagle's Wings" from the contemporary Christian tradition, to a couple of Hebrew songs and Negro spirituals, to "I've Got Peace Like a River," the Beatles' "Let It Be," and Bob Dylan's "Blowin' in the Wind" (which we sang later in the service). The singing of such songs could have been corny or otherwise embarrassing had the band not been so talented and engaging. Once again, however, I lamented the absence of musical notes. Demographically, I fall at the very tail end of the boomer generation, so I had heard these songs before (though not for many years). Most younger visitors would lack any familiarity with them.

Though there was no Christian sung liturgy and no bread and wine communion, the pattern of the service felt familiar, with its sequence of song, announcements, readings, special music, meditation, offering, and closing blessing. For the inspirational reading, a woman named Chris read some of her poems, including one about the "little engine who should." The poem's message about the need to "derail" the "shoulds" in our lives audibly struck a chord with the assembly.

From the announcements and service participants, I gathered that a high percentage of members are artists of one ilk or another. The congregation obviously boasts a number of talented musicians, which earned the Celebration several merit points on my scorecard. For one special musical selection, an a cappella quartet sang "When It's All Been Said and Done." A second song, titled "Tree," was written and sung by Christopher, an accomplished guitarist. He was backed up by three other members who sang harmony as if they'd rehearsed more than just that morning. Everyone sang musically, unself-consciously, and to enthusiastic appreciation.

The human voice also played a role in the day's meditation, which was led by Diana, who wore an understated taupe dress beneath an artistic shawl jacket. Diana, I later learned, had moved from Sedona, Arizona, to Santa Fe two years earlier. I found the Sedona connection unsurprising after the "sound meditation" she presented.

As Diana approached the microphone, she stepped inside what appeared to be a ring of copper wire. Before she started chanting, she place two, smaller rings of wire around her head. Most people closed their eyes as she told them to breathe in "celestial prana through the top of your head" and "terrestrial prana" through the feet. *Prana* means "life-breath," but the word evokes Eastern spiritual practices, so it sounds much more powerful than just "breath." As Diana vocalized, she held a clear crystal—a sure sign of New Age practices—between her mouth and the microphone. I've never been sold on the belief that crystals have healing or other supernatural powers, but if I bring my rational mind to the idea, the notion of crystals possessing or transmitting power isn't so far-fetched. The inner workings of my computer depend on very tiny crystals that might as well be magical for as much as I understand their workings. Countless substances in the natural world form crystals that have various properties that science has exploited. I guess for me the documentary evidence of "New Age" crystals is missing. But maybe I've just not been hanging out with the people who can provide that evidence.

Back within a realm I do understand—music. At one point Diana asked everyone to hum a particular pitch—middle C—while she chanted unidentifiable syllables around that pitch. Most members seemed to be taking it all seriously, following instructions. Perhaps I was too much in the analytical, recording mode to experience the moment as transformative.

The "spirit" in spiritual—rather than the dogma in a given theology—was also at the heart of the day's formal message. Christine Warren's twenty-minute talk on change was less like a sermon than a workshop presentation. Over sandals and a pair of sage chinos she wore a semisheer, feminine blouse that could have been purchased at Judy's on Canyon Road. The look was relaxed but chic Santa Fe. Her long, graying, curly hair framed a face that showed her age but also a beauty that comes with inner peace. Warren's voice was calm and almost trance-inducing; her gestures were fluid and graceful, as you'd expect of a fifty-three-year-old Tesuque yoga master.

She asked us first to get in touch with some change or shift in our lives by closing our eyes and then looking at that change from the perspective of our aged, white-haired selves sitting on our portals and reviewing our lives. Toward the end of this meditation, she asked us to place our hands in prayer position and give thanks for the change. It struck me that, whereas in most Christian congregations you rarely see hands folded in a formal prayer position, in practices such as yoga and the varieties of meditation influenced by Eastern religions, there's much placing of one's hands in prayer position over the heart.

Warren's talk was liberally seasoned with quotations from Carlos Castaneda, Winston Churchill, Henry David Thoreau, Kabir, and the Talmud. The effect was not only to show her as widely read but to demonstrate that the advice she was giving crossed time and cultures. She quoted Thoreau as saying, "Things don't change; we do." From the Talmud: "Things are not as they are. Things are as we are." (My editorial: Substitute "God is" for "Things are" and you have an explanation of how all religions came to be: God is not as "He" is. God is as we are.)

We usually want to hurry past change, to get beyond it, Warren observed, because it can be painful when we outgrow "old forms" and, sometimes, "beloved, good people." But in the first stage of change what we really need to do, she said, is to "put our arms around it" and embrace it. She gave the example of going on retreat for two weeks after divorcing her first husband. During that time she mourned the breakup, even though she had initiated it, and she made lists of all the good things about their ten-year union. Through that example she demonstrated that one tool for getting through change is gratitude. Another is acknowledging the lessons you've learned.

During her talk, I had been thinking of all the obvious changes in my life over the previous year: moving to a different city and state, making a new home livable, working remotely, going through surgery, and discovering and practicing Reiki. While writing about her talk, I was struck with yet another change: my relationship with my spiritual life and religion. In a sense, this book is a demonstration of the process Warren described. In deciding to undertake this project, I was embracing the fact that I was facing a major change in how I related to worship and my spiritual life. I was leaving a stage during which I had been very active in helping to create a worship environment through music. Because David and I hadn't yet found a geographically convenient Lutheran congregation that provided the sort of worship experience we were seeking, I was feeling somewhat cut off from a long, deep, and rich affiliation with my birth church. By comparing the worship experiences I encountered in Santa Fe with the best I'd experienced in the Lutheran church, I was acknowledging lessons learned and, at least indirectly, expressing gratitude for them.

R&R—retreat and reflection, which Warren depicted as "being in the mystery of not knowing where we are"—is another important aspect of navigating change. In our culture, the first question upon meeting someone new is likely to be, "What do you do?" It's not socially acceptable to answer, "I'm working on myself" (except, she noted, in Santa Fe!) or to say, "I'm a chaotic mess at the moment." But out of that surrender to the mystery of not knowing can come a vision, an effortless revelation of a new path that can lead to the joy of declaring that we are, or are "doing," something new.

Warren concluded by having us close our eyes one more time and, though I don't recall the specific instructions she gave, I do remember that she read another passage from Kabir: "Do what you must with another human being, but never put them out of your heart." As soon as these words were uttered, we heard a woman weeping anguished tears. I suspected that the weeper was the woman who, during the "personal sharing" toward the end of the service, gave thanks for another member who had helped on the previous evening to crumble a wall that had stood between them for four years.

Personal sharing time was supposed to be an opportunity to offer a story or announcement with a spiritual dimension. We heard from a man who had lost two-thirds of the weight he was seeking to lose and who had recently been "reinventing" himself as an artist and had just been invited to participate in an art show at Santa Fe's Museum of Fine Arts. A woman originally from Australia told about a recent visit from her newly bereaved brother-in-law. Through heartfelt talks about her deceased sister, they had grown closer than she had thought possible. She asked the community for its prayers for her brother-in-law, a "New Zealand bloke," for whom his newfound spiritual and emotional vulnerability was a radical departure. An elderly woman told a story of serendipity before making a request, on behalf of another member, for house-sitting help. One of the song leaders announced that he had just accepted an unexpected invitation to teach conversational English in China for a year and that he was leaving in a week. Diana announced that her furniture, which had been in storage for two years, had just arrived and that, to celebrate, the Celebrationists were invited the following week to a brunch at her house. She and others asked that everyone send love to residents of Florida, who had recently endured multiple hurricanes.

From this element of the service alone, it was clear that the community practiced what it preached about being "a group of people committed to opening our hearts to all life, all people, all paths, and learning to embrace everything, everyone[,] and especially ourselves[,] in unconditional love. We are committed to doing this in the context of true community, which includes total safety for everyone to be exactly who they are, with their dreams, aspirations, desires, and contributions in the group process."

Visitors were welcomed just before the sharing and were invited to introduce themselves. I was one of two who spoke. I simply gave my first name, said I was visiting a number of Santa Fe faith communities, and explained that this had seemed like a good day to visit the Celebration.

After an offering collection, the service ended with what congregants called a candlelight communion. As the band played and members sang, everyone filed up to the circular table at the front on which burned four white tapers behind four flat bowls of sand. Each person chose a finger-size taper from the adjacent bowls, lit it from one of the full-size candles, and then placed it in the sand. Most people stood with the lit candle in their hands for a moment, in prayer or dedication. Some raised the candle above their head before setting it in the concentric circles that had been drawn in the sand. Then each person joined the chain of singers around the room. It was very much like the closing ritual at Unity Santa Fe. The difference here was that no words were projected onto a screen, so newcomers like myself were on our own to follow the song leaders in a medley of tunes including "Eagle's Wings," "This Little Light of Mine," and the "Alleluia" round.

"We realize that each of us is in fact a sacred part of the Oneness of Everything, which is to say a part of God, and beyond this we endorse no particular creed or dogma." So ends the community's self-description in its bulletin. Given the political and military ends to which creed and dogma have been put over the centuries, the Celebrationists' position seems a highly sane and spiritually evolved one to take.

Yet when you embrace all paths and privilege none, you give up a certain intensity of flavor. For example, at the end of the announcements, Herb noted that the day before had been Yom Kippur, but as someone who had probably been raised in the Jewish traditions, did he miss the observances leading up to the Jewish fes-

tival? And what about Christmas? The song binder didn't include
any Christmas carols, so did Celebrationists add those in December
or simply make an announcement on the last Sunday of December
that Christmas had just passed?

And what about weddings and funerals and births? With no
"ordained" leader, who officiated at such landmark events? What
message was pronounced at a funeral?

The borrowing of practices from various traditions also is presented mostly without context. Diana's sound meditation, for example, included the use of a crystal and unidentifiable syllables. Did the
syllables have any meaning for the chanter? I would have liked to
know.

What would a child learn from this pastiche about any of the
contributing traditions? I think that the piecemeal approach might
leave one feeling a bit groundless. But then maybe that's the point.
Maybe what the Celebration has done is to cull the best elements—
those that ring true to its members today—from varied traditions
and, by amalgamating them, created a picture of God, if you will,
and a multilayered spiritual practice that seeks to address the spiritual longing and experience of twenty-first-century Santa Feans.

The Celebration is uniquely Santa Fe. It takes its inspiration
from the principles in M. Scott Peck's *The Different Drum:
Community Making and Peace* and from Barry Morley's *Beyond
Consensus: The Sense of the Meeting.* It is, as far as I can tell, the only
faith community operating under that name and is affiliated with no
other congregation or organizing body. There's something refresh-
ingly honest in that, as all denominations and worship practices
evolve out of some felt need at a given place and time.
Unfortunately, too many denominations and their practices are
stuck in those originating places and times, so they ignore the reali-
ties of twenty-first-century Earth rather than trying to evolve and lis-

ten to what the Spirit may be trying to tell them today about Truth with a capital T.

If I were a sociologist, it would be interesting to conduct a longitudinal study of the Celebration to see how it evolves (or doesn't) over the next decades. Today, it seems to be the closest practical expression of radical ecumenism that I've heard of.

Can the ecumenism—the recognition that all spiritual paths have something to teach us—plus the dedication to mutual respect and the acknowledgment that all creation is part of one spirit be reconciled with my desire for a sense of tradition, religious heritage, and at least the occasional experience of some ineffably wonderful Bach organ music? Maybe I'm germinating a concept for "my" own religion—the ideal-to-me combination of ritual, theology, and artistic expression. Obviously, new religious communities continue to spawn. Sometimes, yes, they arise out of a "leader's" egotistical or manipulative designs, but just as often they germinate from a sincere desire to acknowledge, experience, and praise the divine.

One way to think about the difference between faith and religion is that religion is what you get when you try to define the practice of faith in some particular way (even if that's a relatively amorphous way, as with the Celebration) and persuade others to join your club.

The more I thought about this congregation, the more I admired its dedication to the idea of an inclusive community run by consensus, because the existence of hierarchy in religion has been the crux of its evils in many cases.

A week later, as I was shopping at Whole Foods, John Lennon's "Imagine" played over the sound system. I stopped my cart for a moment and smiled to myself at yet another Santa Fe serendipity. A couple of evenings earlier, David and I had watched a DVD of the Beatles' first American tour. More significantly, the song reminded me of an essay I had written for a high school religion class. I haven't a clue what the theme was, but I remember two things about that essay. The pastor who taught the course gave me an A and asked me, after class, if he could keep the paper. This was in precomputer days, so it was my only copy. I said no (and then, I'm sure, tossed it in the trash before graduating). Though I don't remember the assigned topic nor my thesis, I do remember that I quoted lyrics from "Imagine," including the line about imagining no religions. The Celebration, it seemed to me, was pursuing a possible path toward creating a faith community without the hard core that can turn religion into a weapon.

NIMATULLAHI SUFI ORDER
SEPTEMBER 27, 2004

"Hello?"

"Hello. I'm calling about the Sufi service listed in the paper—to get an address."

"Do you have any experience with Sufism?"

"No, I'm just visiting a number of different faith communities in Santa Fe."

"Are you doing a survey of some kind?"

"Just a personal survey."

"We generally like to have people read some material before they come. Are you familiar with this order?"

"No, I just found it listed on the religion page."

"Well, I guess you're welcome to come," said the man with a slight Middle Eastern accent, and then he gave me the correct meeting times and address.

"Is there a Web site I could visit for the kind of background reading you had in mind?"

"There's nothing comprehensive on the Web, but you could put in the word 'Nimatullahi' and that will give you some information on the order."

So I did.

Sufism is the mystical branch of Islam. It has an extensive lexicon that suggests a detailed theology and religious practice that I'm sure would be far beyond my ability to make sense of in short order.

But that's not why I wanted to visit. I had started down this road as a church-hopper, a casual visitor who was checking out the vibes at various addresses. I wanted to challenge my preconceptions. I was determined to not turn this into an academic comparative religion book. I was interested in seeing how other faith groups conducted their regular assemblies. I wanted to see what I'd been missing and what I could learn and, possibly, bring into my own experience of Lutheranism to enrich it. I planned to write essays about the experience in the tradition of Montaigne—watching my mind making observations and connections.

Still . . . the more I thought about my conversation with the Sufi, the more reasons I gave myself to skip this hop. I really would be clueless. I didn't have time to read a lot about this order, let alone Sufism in general, and doing so before a visit would just create more preconceptions. I might be the only woman (I was going to make David come with me on this leg of my tour). I suspected the address was a residential one, and I thought I would feel uncomfortable visiting someone's house. Because I'd have no way to participate, I'd stick out as much as if I were to enter their gathering wearing a dozen crosses around my neck. Unlike most of the other assemblies I'd visited, I speculated that the numbers would be small, so there'd be no chance of fading into the back pews.

After a couple of weeks' intermittent reflection, I decided to skip the Sufis. When you're bar-hopping you leave out certain establishments for any number of reasons—one of them being time limitations. In this case, though the fellow I'd spoken to was welcoming toward the end of our conversation, I felt as if I'd be intruding on their private religious practice. At least I can say that the Sufis didn't seem interested in proselytizing.

Given the variety of worship experiences even within a single denomination, I'd never be able to canvass the entire universe of religious communities in Santa Fe. Yet I continued to think about the Sufis. It seemed they had a rather rigorously codified version of religious mysticism. That didn't appeal to me. The famous mystics in any tradition, as far as I knew, hadn't adhered to a preexisting template for accessing their mystical experiences.

But then again, how could I omit a visit to a branch of Islam, when current world events were so intertwined with that religion?

I was almost ready to visit the Sufis when a different point of view on the decision finally percolated through my consciousness: You fool. You're focusing on yourself and your potential discomfort. This guy was probably questioning you because he wonders if you're a government spook. Unfortunately, we live in a country in which some religions more than others have become the object of the government's prying, spying eyes—all in the name of protecting us from terrorism.

From that realization emerged compassion. If I did visit the Sufis, I would do so after I finished this book. After I'd had time to do some reading. After I was ready to experience a sliver of their world for purely personal reasons—not for the sake of including them in this book because Islam happened to be a timely topic.

CHRIST CHURCH,
PRESBYTERIAN CHURCH IN AMERICA
OCTOBER 3, 2004

Because I'm a sucker for interesting graphic design, especially the artful use of typography, a quarter-page ad in *Pasetiempo, The New Mexican's* weekend arts and entertainment supplement, caught my attention and inspired me to visit Christ Church— even though I'd already visited a Presbyterian church.

The ad's body copy was set in a cruciform shape. Though I can't replicate the actual type styles and sizes and the mix of lowercase plus full-size and small caps, the text read:

O Heavenly
Redeemer
Let us rejoice
And celebrate
Christ
Transforming
Community
Ancient & indigenous
Christ Church
Paleo-Orthodox
Liberating
Grace
Authenticity
Ethos
Pathos
Logos
In the beginning

Was the Word
and the word was
God.

Underneath the church's logo were the words "Clarity Mystery Incarnation" and the image of a skeleton key. At the bottom, in the smallest type of all, the church was identified as belonging to the Presbyterian Church in America (PCA). That raised some suspicions: Was it trying to pass itself off as something other than Presbyterian?

When I mentioned the ad to Tom, my Lutheran pastor brother-in-law, and his wife, Diane, they guessed that, with its artsy ad, Christ Church was trying to appeal to a younger and a gay demographic that they described as being into "smells and bells." In other words, they expected "high church" worship with incense and an aerobic workout of liturgical gesturing.

Boy, were we all wrong.

To pull the mask off the mystery, I sacrificed a perfectly beautiful fall morning to visit the congregation. No incense, no genuflecting. Definitely no gay or lesbian couples.

This is not the Presbyterian Church (USA), as is First Pres in downtown Santa Fe. Like Baptists and Lutherans, Presbyterians come in more than one flavor. According to the PCA's official Web site, it split from mainline Presbyterians in 1973 in reaction to the Presbyterians' perceived liberalism, their stance on the scriptures, and giving women a full role in the life of the church. PCAs, in contrast, hold to the so-called traditional position of women in the church—that is, a second-class, nonpastoral role. Though the PCA defines itself as "reformed" on its Web site and as paleo-orthodox in the Christ Church ad, the latter is just a twenty-dollar word for what most people would call fundamentalist or literalist.

The service and handouts provided no elucidation of the "paleo-orthodox" moniker. In trying to uncover what the term might mean for Christ Church, I found several online references to a Center for the Advancement of Paleo-Orthodoxy (CAPO). Unfortunately, the CAPO Web site was unavailable because it was "undergoing a facelift." CAPO is one of the organizations listed as advocating the antiseparation of church and state. Among its activities is sponsorship of political and economic think tanks, including the Kuyper Institute.

Christ Church's brochure explains that it's a missional church. "Therefore we communicate the Gospel to Santa Fe by adapting and reformulating all we do in worship, discipleship, community and service in order to connect with the non-Christian culture around us with both the transcendent glory of God and the nearness of God in the Gospel." Their ad's clever graphic design must be part of that "adapting and reformulating," but a fundie church is still a fundie church that shuts its eyes to all truth that falls outside proscribed boundaries and that forbids women to be clergy. And to call Santa Fe a non-Christian culture? For longer than any other American community, this city has been at least nominally Christian, starting with the Spanish priests and colonizers. Historically, you can't get much more Christian. Today there are probably more Christian churches per capita in Santa Fe than in most American cities.

However, I didn't know all that about the PCA even after I'd attended one of its services, which highlights the limitations of church-hopping: You can't always get a comprehensive read of a congregation's theology, culture, and spirit from a single service.

Christ Church met in an open, sunlit dining hall at the Community College of Santa Fe. Tucked into the white stuccoed corner formed by a V-shaped divider wall were the musicians: two singing guitarists, a fiddler, a singer sans instrument, and a bongo player. Behind them was a Spanish-style wood-and-tin cross. In front of them stood a small white lectern and a portable altar with flowers and communion elements. Stacking chairs for at least three hundred were arranged in a semicircle facing the altar.

I thought I was going to be a bit late, but the noise level told me I wasn't. Young children ran around, adults gathered in small groups around the coffee table and among the chairs. This congregation had a full complement of kids, from babies to high schoolers. Even the adult median age was lower than at most mainline Protestant churches. They were doing something right to attract the prime demographic.

An a capella white gospel prelude, "Talk about Sufferin," was well sung by four of the musicians. For the congregational songs, half had words and melody printed in the bulletin, but half offered words only. Though I was grateful for the notes, the musicians did not always play in the key that was printed, which was disconcerting. However, the song of praise, "Thy Mercy My God Is the Theme," went up to a high A in the printed version, so lowering the key was a good move. That tune had a slightly bluegrass feeling to it that was accentuated by a fiddle obbligato. When the jeans-wearing fiddler switched to a mandolin for the offertory, "Eternity in Our Hearts," I thought to myself, "Yup, he's a bluegrass player."

With the exception of the unaccompanied solo chants during communion—one in Latin, the other in English—the musical genre is what I'd call contemporary Christian country ballad. The uniformity of tempo and musical affect made for a consistent but ultimately dull musical experience.

Fortyish Rev. Logan Craft led the service up to the sermon, giving announcements, leading prayers, and reading lessons. He wore a blue jacket, striped blue shirt without a tie, tan pants, and dark brown suede tassel loafers. His straight dark hair was slicked back, his mustache carefully trimmed.

There was time after the first song for folks to greet each other, and I exchanged good mornings with the attractive and charming young couple sitting next to me. Their two-year-old spent most of the service in the nursery. I was happy that visitors weren't put on the spot. It seemed like a warm, friendly community.

After the blessing of the children, the bulletin announced "Holy Silence" during which we were invited to "slow down, pray or think on your relationship with God." Great idea. Crummy execution. Rev. Craft began with a litany of prayers and then announced the silence, but at that point we were standing. Now, anyone who knows anything about meditation knows that it's better achieved while sitting—or even walking. Not only were we standing, but the silence lasted ten seconds max. That's not enough time for three deep, cleansing breaths! I think I know why churches such as this one give only lip service to silence, meditation, and the mystical. It's because if they actually honored meditation, they'd have to open themselves to the possibility of personal insight—of spiritual revelation and experience that's extra-doctrinal.

Senior Pastor Martin Ban, aka the bongo player, delivered the sermon. Just before his talk, however, he introduced a fellow pastor, Skip, and his wife, Amy, with whom he had served in Kansas City. The couple had just returned from serving as missionaries to a Muslim community near Barcelona, Spain. Skip claimed that Spain was only two percent Christian and that twice that percentage of Spaniards identified themselves as Satanists. Then he talked about a Muslim man who had converted and changed his name in recognition of his religious change.

Though he referred to his two teenagers and one preteen child, Rev. Ban had a youthful look that may have been assisted by his wire-rimmed glasses and short goatee. I was starting to see a pattern in clergy apparel: mainline Catholic and Protestant officiants wear ornamental liturgical robes; fundamentalist and alternative Christian clergy stick to street clothes.

Ban wore an open-necked patterned shirt under a brown tweedy jacket. Beneath his tan pants, cowboy boots stuck out. Was his a costume calculated to appeal to Santa Fe sensibilities? Or had he moved from Kansas City and the Pacific Northwest and simply fallen in love with "Western" apparel?

Ban's sermon was based on the text from Luke 7 in which the story is told of Jesus bringing a widow's dead son back to life. I was looking forward to the sermon, because the Luke story is one of healing. However, unbelievable as this sounds, Ban didn't focus on the healing or resuscitation (why not say resurrection?) of the boy.

He prefaced his sermon with an anecdote about overhearing a teenagers' youth group discussion in which the kids determined that all questions posed in Sunday School could be responded to with one of the following three answers: "Love God," "Jesus," or "Pray." Then he asked his listeners to become "charmingly cynical" teenagers for a few minutes. As such, Rev. Ban said, we might ask, "What's the point of raising this guy if he's just going to die later on?" The answer, he explained had more to do with the grieving mother than the son, because in Jewish culture at that time, a widowed mother with no other male in her family would have been economically destitute. So it was compassion not only for her grief but also for her physical circumstances that led Jesus to voluntarily raise her child from the dead, Ban said.

He also spoke about the pain that grieving parents feel, about a child whose funeral he had officiated at, about how C.S. Lewis's struggles with the fact that death never seems natural led him to Christianity, about how "there's nothing more practical than hope"—though Ban didn't provide evidence to bolster that claim. In manner, this pastor was quite charming. He didn't rant and rave like a wind-up evangelist, though he was clearly evangelistic. He spoke a language his parishioners understood, and he addressed real life-and-death issues. From just that one sermon, I could even have thought he was a Lutheran pastor.

At the end of the ninety-minute service, Rev. Ban led a short congregational meeting at which those present adopted a resolution to petition the regional presbytery that they become a "particular," self-governing and self-supporting church rather than a mission church. After the motion passed unanimously, an elderly man gave a closing prayer. He took a few moments to compose himself, but even after he began speaking, it was clear he was fighting through emotions to give thanks for the congregation's growth, its blessings, and its first steps toward becoming a full-fledged church. I mention the man's prayer because his emotions seemed real; he must believe in what the church stands for and must hold that dear to his heart.

I have conflicted feelings about Christ Church. Like the Church of Christ, it purports to practice an authentic Christianity that hews to what Jesus taught. It seems such a simple and pure claim, but I have less faith in the transparency of early Christianity than those two congregations have (especially as they don't go back to the earliest Christianity, whose practices incorporated women as more equal partners in the community's work, as historians including Elaine Pagels have shown). I felt tricked by Christ Church's marketing tactics, which cloak its literalist, antifeminist doctrine in artsy advertising and "local color" music in order to seduce unsuspecting wanderers into an apparently friendly fold. Yet as a defender of religious freedom, I can't fault them for their marketing savvy.

TEMPLE BETH SHALOM
OCTOBER 22, 2004

Shabbat Shalom!

Shabbat Shalom!

That call and response, "Welcome Sabbath," opened and closed Friday evening prayers at Temple Beth Shalom. In between, most of the nineteen pieces of the service were sung or chanted in Hebrew.

At first, I tried to follow along, but there were no notes to tell me the rhythm and duration of the syllables. Pronouncing the Hebrew words themselves was a task I proved inept at, so I quickly abandoned all hope of participating in the service. Instead, I glanced at the three versions of texts—the Hebrew script, its transliteration, and the English translation—but then focused on the sounds.

As in the Greek Orthodox service, I felt as if I'd stepped back in time. In marked contrast to the Greek service, though, this one felt full of joy. There was a buzz of friendly chatter among the two hun-dred-some attendees before service started, and much of the music was lively, inspiring smiles and movement. As the instrumentalists introduced the first song and congregants began swaying and tapping their feet, I heard another visitor say, "It's like a Jewish wedding!"

In the front right corner of the sanctuary, the musicians were led by a gray-haired man who played guitar and piano. Behind him were two older men, one on double bass, another on accordion. They were flanked by a younger man playing clarinet and a woman play-ing a silver hand drum that resembled a communion chalice laid on its side with a drum skin over its mouth. For the first song, a female clarinetist joined the ensemble. The clarinets in particular defined the ensemble's sound. At a couple of points in the service the accordionist and clarinetist took short solos. In virtuosity, one of the clarinet interludes resembled a rhapsody.

I didn't know the melodies and couldn't sing along, but I could and did move my feet. How could one not?

A member of the adult mitzvah class lit two candles at the beginning of the service. The prayer book explained that they represented the two commandments about the Sabbath: to remember it and keep it.

The service had the rhythm of vespers, with a song, short prayers, chants, then more song. Sometimes the female song leader was joined at the altar by two young women who added soprano harmonies. Though most of the regulars in the pews participated, at times their singing got a little frayed around the edges. The pulse and pitch would stray, but with the return of a refrain or familiar passage, they'd circle back to the center of the melody.

I'd been in the congregation's sanctuary before, for *The Passion of the Christ* dialog, but this was the first time I'd attended a Jewish service. So it came as a surprise that the prayer book is printed backwards—with the back cover serving as the "front" and pages numbered from back to front. (A Web site for Temple Beth Shalom in Cambridge, Massachusetts, explained that books written in Hebrew are printed with page numbers running "backwards" because Hebrew is written from right to left.)

Though I wouldn't know until later in the service who they were, seven adult Hebrew students were seated at the front left of the sanctuary. The two men and five women all wore prayer shawls. The following morning they would chant the Torah as the culmination of their two-year tutelage. I inferred from comments made by the women that the class was probably composed of individuals who had been raised as secular Jews and who had decided to become religious Jews by participating in this right of passage. In place of a message from Rabbi Schwab, two of the women and one of the men gave brief presentations.

I sat in the de facto visitors' corner, the back corner closest to the exit doors. To my right was a fair-haired couple who didn't speak a word to me or utter a word during the service. They gave me a faint smile as I passed in front of them to claim a seat but not such a generous one as to invite conversation. It was a manner I recognized. I myself had adopted it repeatedly over the past months: If I sit quietly in the back and don't draw attention to myself, maybe nobody will make me say anything publicly.

To my left were two short, elderly Jewish ladies. They, too, were visiting, but they knew all the texts and most of the music. At one point in the service I noticed that the one next to me was reading the original Hebrew—her hand covered the Arabic letters of the song being sung.

In front of us were two other visiting couples. The Hispanic couple stood out even more than I. The mystery of their presence was lifted when visitors were invited to introduce themselves; they were there to support one of the adult students. Beside them sat a couple of talkative Jewish women who made clear from their comments that they were first-time visitors. Two-thirds of the way through the service, one said to the other, "I haven't heard a word of English yet. I'd like to hear *some* English."

English was used only in the announcements, some of the prayers, and the students' presentations. History and tradition rather than contemporary concerns were preeminent in the song and prayer texts, which praised God and petitioned for protection and peace.

No offering was taken that evening, so I wondered what the routine was for generating financial support. There was also, obviously, no Christian communion, though there was a blessing of wine and bread. With the adult students surrounding him at the altar, Rabbi Schwab drank from the cup and broke and shared the challah bread with his students.

The other obvious ceremonial part of the liturgy involved the rabbi sliding open a screen behind the altar to reveal several books on scrolls—the Torah, I assumed. With the altar and students between me and the scrolls, I couldn't see or hear what was being done.

I felt a little stupid. Here I was, a lifelong Christian, highly educated, and even a graduate of high school- and college-level religion courses, yet I couldn't interpret the most basic elements of Jewish worship. I'd received a Christian education—not a religious one. Though this church-touring escapade lacked the depth of study required of comparative religious education, at least it was a step along that road. At least it clued me in to how much I don't know.

I had saved the Jewish community for last because my Lutheran Christian background derives, ultimately, from Judaism. Though I'd always felt that, as a Christian, I had more in common with Jews than with people of other faiths because we share sacred books and worship the same God, I realized that Friday in October that our traditions are in other ways worlds apart and that I disrespected Judaism by conceiving of it as simply the ancestor of Christianity.

The first woman who stood up to talk about her adult Jewish education journey glowed with happiness and shared thanks for the support of family and friends. As she spoke of the community she'd become part of at Temple Beth Shalom, I thought about how many people join a Jewish synagogue or a Christian church or a Zen mediation group as a way of meeting people. When I was a senior in high school, the mother of a good friend of mine told me that she'd suggested to her son that he join a church in the city to which he'd moved so he could meet people. I remember thinking it odd that she would give that advice. Though their family was one of the kindest I knew, they weren't church-goers. For me there would have to be more to the choice of a faith community.

The second woman said that because she was raised in a nonobservant Jewish household, she felt different but not special. Halfway through her presentation, tears choked her voice as she recounted how, as one of ten Jews in a middle school class of one hundred and fifty, she had been taunted. Both Rabbi Schwab and a member seated near the front rose to hand her tissues. As she thanked family members for their support, she mentioned a daughter and her partner. "Another one!" the auburn-haired woman in front of me said as she elbow-jabbed the woman next to her.

The male student spoke of his Torah selection and his mitzvah project, as the others had. But what was most memorable was how he justified his project, which involved generating support for a multimillion-dollar investment in telecommunications infrastructure for the state. Without it, he said, young New Mexicans would miss out on the economic opportunities that such infrastructure would make possible and would, instead, be prepared only to "flip burgers and make babies." The woman in front of me was shocked and said to her companion, "That's insulting. I'm going to say something to him about that afterward."

Though I'd been captivated by the palpable joy at Temple Beth Shalom, clearly this congregation was no different than any other in one respect: It was composed of individuals who can't help but bring their whole selves—prejudices, inadequacies, and frailties—into the community's conversation and life. Yet they find common ground in the words and sounds and gestures of the Jewish liturgy, which have sustained so many for so long. Perhaps that's one of the saving graces of any worship service: It can temporarily suspend individual pettiness and self-centeredness while giving us a glimpse of what it might mean to live in community as God's people, focused on the bigger picture.

THE RAPTURE
AND APOCALYPTIC SCRIPTURE
OCTOBER 24, 2004

I could have spent another eight months visiting places of worship in Santa Fe and not retraced my steps, but comprehensiveness wasn't my purpose. This project started as a diversion from my previous routine of being tied to one congregation every Sunday. Almost immediately, it germinated into an idea for a book. Along the way it became a more personal, serious exploration of what I believe and why (not all the details of which are contained in these pages). But how to know when to quit? As in the beginning, so in the end, spirit guided me.

When I learned that the Santa Fe Jewish and Christian Dialogue was sponsoring a forum on the rapture and apocalyptic scripture, I thought, What better way to end than with an event focusing on the "end times"?

Temple Beth Shalom hosted the gathering. It was timely, coming just a week before the 2004 presidential election. Those who believe in the rapture expect it to consist of the whisking away of born-again Christians into heaven. (Just where do they think that is? Somewhere beyond our galaxy? Beyond where astronomers have been able to see?) That's to happen before the second coming of Christ, which is to be preceded by a period of earthly horrors for those "left behind." More important, some of those believers think they should be involved in expediting the rapture by seeing to it that what they interpret as precursors to the rapture—war, famine, plague, earthquake—actually come about. For some such people, war with Middle Eastern countries, with Islam, is a good thing.

Though I've never heard the rapture mentioned in a Lutheran church, anticipating that moment is a central tenet of many fundamentalist/literalist Christian theologies. Over the millennia, since the earliest apocalyptic books were written, visions of the final days have failed to be made manifest. Even if you take just the book of Revelation in the New Testament, the number of times that people or religious bodies have predicted a fulfillment of John's vision is staggering, yet no one has correctly predicted the date. And therein lies the problem: Apocalyptic scriptures are prophetic, not predictive, as the forum's speakers explained.

After earning a Harvard Ph.D., Hindy Najman, the first speaker, taught at Notre Dame University for six years before becoming an associate professor of Near and Middle Eastern civilizations and religions at the University of Toronto. M. Eugene Boring, professor of New Testament at Texas Christian University in Fort Worth, is the author of several books, including *Revelation, Interpretation: A Bible Commentary for Teaching and Preaching.*

Najman began by talking about the long tradition of prophetic literature in the Jewish tradition and provided a handout of excerpts from some of that literature: 1 Enoch, Jubilees, Dead Sea Scrolls and 4 Ezra. Though enormously learned, her presentation style leaned toward stream of consciousness, and it was evident that she frequently spoke well above the audience members' threshold of understanding. Nevertheless, she made some essential points about this genre of sacred literature.

Revelation was written in the context of crisis. Its author, a man named John (but not the John whose name is given to the New Testament gospel of John), was imagining a better place, beyond his present, in which death could be the consequence of professing Jesus as Lord. Najman explained that in this period of history, Jews and the people who would later be called Christians held shared concepts about the nature of God and the end time. Apocalyptic literature was a way of overcoming trauma, as one audience member put it. It's part of the poetic imagination, Najman said, occupying the space between the human and the divine. In other words, in no sense was apocalyptic literature seen in its own time as predicting a literal future for some definable time.

Before Boring's presentation, we watched a videotaped *60 Minutes* segment in which Morley Saffer opened by pointing to Americans' enormous interest in the idea of the rapture. That interest has been fueled in part by fiction about the rapture, the twelve-part *Left Behind* book series. The *60 Minutes* episode also ran clips of a movie about the rapture in which the "saved" disappear from cars and airplanes, leaving only their clothes behind. Saffer interviewed several Christians who believe in the rapture and, finally, the chaplain of Harvard University, Rev. Professor Peter J. Gomes (and author of *The Good Book: Reading the Bible with Mind and Heart*), who discredited their view. The rapturists who were interviewed said they believed that not just the Jewish Saffer but even other Christians, those who don't "accept Jesus Christ as their personal savior," would not be saved in the rapture but would be left to endure the earthly scourges that would follow.

It was a stunning example of how exclusionary and hubristic some brands of Christianity can be.

Boring introduced his presentation as concerning the political relevance of Revelation. With his white hair and glasses, he looked the role of the professor, but he also understood that his audience wanted an explication of this controversial text that they could make sense of in their lives.

His handout used as an epigraph this quotation: "I am not concerned about dogmas, but I don't tolerate a pulpit pounder getting involved in earthly matters" (Adolf Hitler). Boring's point was that Hitler recognized—as Jews always have, and as many Christian groups in this country now do—that biblical faith is related to political decisions. Then he made the essential clarification that Revelation has something to say *to* our times, but it does not talk *about* them. The book is political—and anti-empire in its politics.

As does all literature, all apocalyptic literature reflects *its own time*—typically a time of great suffering. Revelation was written about 95 CE, during or just after Nero's time—a period of persecution for the followers of Jesus.

Like a painting, Revelation has to be "experienced," Boring said. The word of God comes *through* the book but it works like a work of art. In contrast to the rapturists' understanding of this text, mainline theological schools agree on the interpretation of Revelation: It is prophetic but not predictive. To understand how and why the last book of the New Testament came to be, Boring noted that it was written within years of 4 Ezra. The people who first read Revelation would have immediately recognized what it was and how it worked, because they were familiar with the genre of Jewish prophetic, apocalyptic literature. They would not have made the mistake of interpreting it as literally predictive of future events—let alone predictive of events in our generation, two millennia hence! Furthermore, the idea of the rapture is nowhere found in the book of Revelation, Boring pointed out. Far from depicting an "escape from history," as Boring put it, Revelation promises "the redemption of history."

We broke after three hours for a catered dinner of gyros and spanakopita. I sat across from a woman who said she went to one of the Episcopal churches in town. She talked with her friend about her son, who had moved to the West Coast and whom she had encouraged to attend church as a way of meeting people. Though her son had been raised Episcopalian, she said she guessed that, according to Revelation, her son would be left behind in the rapture. It was all I could do to keep from yelling across the table at her, "Did you hear nothing that Boring said? He couldn't have been clearer: The rapture is not even hinted at in Revelation. You completely missed the point!" In retrospect, I realize that I shouldn't have let "good manners" get in the way of serving a greater good. I should have tactfully clarified that the notion of the "left behind" was something that interviewees on the *60 Minutes* clip believe, not something that Revelation contains.

What's more, I could have pointed out that all the predictions of apocalyptic literature have been wrong—at least in their timing. If nothing else, that shows that we humans have never been able to fully know the mind of God and that we've failed miserably when we've tried to play God.

During the postdinner question-and-answer session, one woman asked, "How did the rapture movement start? It seems so un-Christian and so unloving." Boring explained that it started with a lawyer named John Nelson Darby, who lived the same time as Darwin's work was challenging literalist interpretations of the Genesis story. Darby, in part attempting to approach the Bible "scientifically," tried to systematize and reorder biblical episodes so they made sense in terms of predicting what we would now call the rapture. The idea of plucking discrete pieces from one part of the Bible and placing them next to other pieces written in different places and times under different circumstances for different reasons and in different genres is ridiculous, as any professional theologian will tell you. Boring recommended Craig Hill's *In God's Time* as a more detailed look at rapture theory and its alternatives.

Interest in an apocalypse was especially strong during the world wars, which were seen as signs of the end time. Every generation, Boring said, that reads the Bible as predictive for its generation has tried to see biblical predictions as applying to its generation—and all the predictions have been wrong. Boring offered this approach to reading the Genesis story, Revelation, and other sacred texts in a way that honors their historical and theological origins, our present reality, and our religious traditions: "We don't take them literally, but we take them seriously."

Both Najman and Boring offered ultimately hopeful visions of the future. In response to a final question, Najman acknowledged that organized religion is "beautiful and ugly . . . like humans are beautiful and ugly and like acts of nature are beautiful and ugly." But, she added, prayer can be used "to lift you out of darkness."

Boring focused on the final vision presented in Revelation. In it, the writer says, "I saw no temple in the city" (Revelation 21:22). Instead of a church, there's a tree in the center of John's imagined city: "on either side of the river, the tree of life with its twelve kinds of fruit, yielding its fruit each month; and the leaves of the tree were for the healing of the nations" (Revelation 22:2). Not a temple nor a church nor a mosque, but the tree of life from the Garden of Eden. No religions, just life and healing of the nations. I leaned over to whisper in David's ear, "Lennon had it right in 'Imagine'!" Two minutes later, as moderator Rev. Holly Beaumont thanked the speakers, she too invoked John Lennon's imagining a time when there'd be no religions but, instead, peace among all people and all nations.

That's a prophetic vision worth praying for.

EPILOGUE

This project—this grand tour of faith communities—began as a lark but evolved into something more serious. How could it not for someone who knows in her heart that there's a power and existence that transcends, but infuses, this physical life? Curiosity, opportunity, and a desire to find a unique way to connect with my new community prompted my research, but I believe I was inspired by what Christians call the Spirit.

When I set off on my church-hopping, I had a number of questions in mind. Though I didn't discover definitive answers to any of them, I did find partial, temporal ones.

As for whether or not Santa Fe is an inherently spiritual place, I have to answer affirmatively. Though I would distinguish between its being a spiritual place and a religious place, the depth of religious influence on the culture, particularly Hispanic culture, has created an environment in which it's not automatically seen as weird to discuss matters of the spirit or the divine.

Religion has been intimately entwined with this city's history. Though it's beyond the scope of this book to recount that history, its effects are visible even today. You can see it in sacred pueblo dances that are open to the public, blurring the line between entertaining spectacle and private rite. Fall's Fiesta, though ostensibly secular and social, ends with a mass in the cathedral.

Both history and an inspiring landscape may have contributed to the flourishing of a greater-than-average variety of religious and spiritual traditions in this place, yet it seems to me that the number of religious institutions is less a sign of this city's spirituality than its openness to that diversity and the greater public respect for that diversity than you might find in some other parts of the country.

That's not to say that other places can't be or become just as spirit friendly. For one thing, anyone can go church-touring (more on that later). Knowledge is better than ignorance, even if you decide that you favor your own tradition over others. Once you start looking for signs of spirit-filled lives, you might find them where you least expected to.

Second, just as bars aren't the only place to get a drink, churches and synagogues and meditation centers aren't the only places to worship, to get a spiritual education, or to grow spiritually. A spiritual place can be the place where you're standing. My sabbatical from regular attendance at the same church confirmed that, for me, time spent reading sacred texts and books about religion and spirituality are as important—maybe more important at this stage in my life—to my spiritual health and growth.

What, then, is the point of "church-going"? Ask a theologian and you'll get one kind of answer. Ask overworked parents of young children and you'll get another. For me, it's an opportunity to acknowledge by being in the presence of others that I'm not alone in believing in the divine, in expressing gratitude for the Spirit's presence in my life, and in seeking ways to respond more fully to that spirit. Ideally, at least, worshipping in even small communities of faith can be a gesture of recognition that each individual is an interdependent part of a divine creation. Churches—at least those that don't seek to control members with fear tactics—can be energizing places for dialog and discovery. Most worship traditions also provide a framework for marking and celebrating the cycles of the year—cycles that are intimately tied to nature's cycles in spite of organized religion's attempts to disassociate itself from "pagan" connections.

✦ ✦ ✦

I was also looking for a spirit of joy. I'm not talking about the good time that a bar-hopper might look for.

There's a line in the Lutheran baptismal liturgy, addressed to God in prayer, that reads: "Pour your Holy Spirit upon [name]: the spirit of wisdom and understanding, the spirit of counsel and might, the spirit of knowledge and the fear of the Lord, the spirit of joy in your presence." I bracket for now the illogic of being fearful of and joyous in the presence of the same entity. What does that "joy in your presence" look like, sound like? Not to fall too far into the well of semantics, but for me, in the context of the divine, joy isn't an exact synonym for happiness. Whereas happiness suggests content- ment, joy contains aspects of gratitude and peace. Happiness is rel- atively passive, whereas joy implies rejoicing—creative energy. Such joy might be made manifest in spirited music-making of the sort I heard at the Celebration or it might be reflected in an ego-less, peaceful demeanor that doesn't draw a lot of attention to itself but that makes the joyous person an ideal spiritual confidante—as it does for a particular Lutheran woman I know.

Though I'd been in plenty of churches with good music and friendly people over the years, the presence of joy is harder to find. And like most extreme emotions, it's often ephemeral. I think I witnessed joy mostly in congregations that made a point of expressing gratitude and that espoused a theology in which the believer was seen as being connected to the divine rather than "separated by sin" from God.

✦ ✦ ✦

Bar-hoppers often have a favorite bar—one where they're a reg- ular. I'm not ready to declare myself a regular at any place I visited, but I have identified some must-haves and won't-tolerates for any place I'd make my regular place of worship.

The element that's guaranteed to turn me around at the door— as smoke does in a bar—a church that requires me to check my brain at the door, that forbids questioning, or that sees "salvation" or enlightenment as something achieved only according to its unbending dictates.

My ideal church's pastor or leader would be reverent and soulful but not stuffy or self-important. Gender is less important than an obvious respect for and inclusion of both sexes in worship and in the church's theology and doctrine.

Service music would be engaging—well chosen and artfully (even if not professionally) led. A pipe organ played by a talented organist would be heavenly, but other instrumental leadership can be just as effective in some settings. Words and music would be supplied for all but the simplest responses. If the term "praise music" were uttered, it would be in reference to something like the "Halleluiah Chorus."

Members would be friendly but not pushy—welcoming but not suffocating. Parishioners would be happy to gather together and would be engaged in worship—especially singing.

A full complement of age groups in the worship service would help everyone remember that, just as members may differ in age, they also may differ in spiritual needs.

In reality, if we want to be church-goers, we make the best of what's at hand and try to spark positive change in the areas we can influence. If we encounter too many aspects of an assembly that stifle our souls rather than helping them expand, we either move to another worship center or abandon organized religion altogether.

I started this journey as a Lutheran. What am I now?

I'll always be Lutheran, just as I'll always be Anglo. But being a regular church-going Lutheran has never been enough. I always knew that; I just didn't give myself permission to seriously explore what my alternatives or additive options were, partly because the

Lutheran Church—like most churches—doesn't encourage members to be both Lutheran and Buddhist or to worship in church on Sunday but meditate with the Zen crowd on Wednesday or attend the Unity service every other week.

I'm extremely grateful that I was born into the more progressive branch of Lutheranism. The Lutheran Church and its educational institutions were the perfect settings in which to develop my love of music. I had the good fortune to become friends with numerous Lutheran pastors and their families who were kind-hearted, intelligent, sincere—and sometimes silly in a wonderfully human way.

But I no longer can be exclusively or narrowly Lutheran.

If it were possible, I would probably declare myself a nondenominational Christian, as M. Scott Peck has done. Peck, who wasn't raised in any religious tradition, was baptized a Christian in what he calls a nondenominational celebration after years of exploring a variety of Eastern and mystical spiritual traditions. Though I may attend Lutheran services, I know that I will continue to seek for and experience spiritual truth in multiple ways.

I can even begin to imagine believing without belonging.

A National Public Radio story on May 10, 2004, looked at how the United States has always been fertile ground for the development of new religions—eight hundred to one thousand by some counts, with twenty new ones formed every year. Though not all new faiths survive, let alone thrive, sociologists argue that the experimentation that happens on the fringes of religion often finds its way into more mainstream practice, as have elements of meditation, for example.

The NPR story continued by noting that the new focus in religion, according to an expert at Canada's University of Waterloo, is "believing without belonging." Disillusionment with corruption and intolerance within established church institutions is just one reason for this attitude. Today, sociologists say, religion must touch the heart and body, which they see as one explanation for the popularity of pentecostal movements. Others find established church doctrine too narrow for their experience of or yearning for the divine. Witness the popularity of Wicca, which espouses no particular doctrine yet connects with many people's concerns about nature and the environment and which acknowledges the feminine dimension of the divine.

NPR's correspondent concluded with the observation that, a long time ago, Christianity was a fringe religion that now is "the largest religious force in the world."

If you've found these pages in any way interesting, I encourage you to take your own tour of faith communities.

That idea may meet with resistance in some corners. Churches have a vested interest in a fixed customer base. It makes budgeting easier, for one thing. I completely sympathize with that desire from the administrative angle. Choosing a single church and sticking with it makes a lot of sense in most situations: if you want to plant deeper roots in a community, meet people and develop friendships based on common interests, or raise children in a familiar and (you hope) safe community, for example.

However, even for worshippers with such motives for membership in a particular faith community, a sabbatical of sorts for exploring other worship traditions can be fruitful. For one thing, upon their return, they could help their home churches examine more practically what it means to be ecumenical, if that is a stated goal. More broadly, a church tour could reconfirm or revise one's tenets of faith.

Some folks may experience an epiphany somewhere along the road, not unlike the apostle Paul's. A lifelong Baptist might discover that he likes the pomp and circumstance of the Catholic tradition—and its shorter sermons—while a Catholic by birth may realize that she's been a Wiccan at heart her whole life.

For clergy or other church leaders wary of this idea or tempted to preach against it, I ask, "What are you afraid of?" Such an exercise can lead to better understanding of the divine and our fellow humans, even if it merely puts faces on the labels we use to talk about other believers. Those who return to their home congregation will likely do so with renewed interest and conviction. Those who leave may well be replaced by others engaged in this tour.

No single denomination—no matter what its leaders tell you—has a patent on the truth, the whole truth, and nothing but the truth. The fundamental problem is that we're all human—as well as divine. Despite claims of divine anointings and apostolic succession, all religious leaders are human, which means they're fallible—some more than others. If it's certainty you're looking for, the only certainty is that you'll find something amiss in every church.

Your spiritual life is too important to turn it over mindlessly and unquestioningly to any religion, denomination, or leader. Ask of any church or guru: What have they got to gain, and what have I got to lose, by adhering to these precepts or worshipping in this environment? Then keep your brain and your spirit plugged in—even if you don't go church-hopping.

For English and, later, American travelers in the eighteenth and nineteenth centuries, education and entertainment were joint motives for making a Grand Tour of Europe. After several months or years abroad, the traveler would usually return home, where, it was assumed, he (more often than she) would be equipped to incorporate a broadened understanding of history, art, and culture into his life and leadership roles.

May your grand tours educate and inspire richer, fuller lives.

NOTES

St. Bede's Episcopal Church, March 7, 2004

3 "As the sun was going down, a deep sleep fell upon Abram, and a deep and terrifying darkness descended upon him." From the Order of Service, St. Bede's Episcopal Church, Santa Fe, New Mexico (March 7, 2004).

The Passion of the Christ, March 8, 2004

9 "And they crucified him, and divided his garments among them, casting lots for them, to decide what each should take" (Mark 15:24). From *The New Oxford Annotated Bible: The Holy Bible,* Revised Standard Version, eds. Herbert G. May and Bruce M. Metzger (New York: Oxford University Press, 1973).

A "New Spirituality"? March 11, 2004

14 "To quote President Kennedy from shortly before he was killed, 'From those to whom much has been given, much is asked.'" The version from Luke 12:48 reads, "Everyone to whom much is given, of him will much be required." From *The New Oxford Annotated Bible: The Holy Bible,* Revised Standard Version, eds. Herbert G. May and Bruce M. Metzger (New York: Oxford University Press, 1973).

First Presbyterian Church, March 14, 2004

17 "Render therefore to Caesar the things that are Caesar's, and to God the things that are God's." Matthew 22:21, *The New Oxford Annotated Bible: The Holy Bible,* Revised Standard Version, eds. Herbert G. May and Bruce M. Metzger (New York: Oxford University Press, 1973).

22 I first became familiar with the Blessing Way Prayer as a Navajo prayer, but it is also used (with variations) by many other faith communities.

First Baptist Church, April 4, 2004
34 Colossians 2:13–14, *The New Oxford Annotated Bible: The Holy Bible,* Revised Standard Version, eds. Herbert G. May and Bruce M. Metzger (New York: Oxford University Press, 1973).

Cathedral Church of St. Francis of Assisi, Easter, April 11, 2004
54 Katharine Q. Seelye, "Kerry Attends Easter Services and Receives Holy Communion," *The New York Times,* electronic edition (April 12, 2004).

Hinduism, April 2004
56 "U.S. Scholar Threatened by Hindu Faithful," reprinted from *The Washington Post* in *The Santa Fe New Mexican* (April 13, 2004).

The Rapture and Apocalyptic Scripture, October 24, 2004
167 All quotes from Revelation from *The New Oxford Annotated Bible: The Holy Bible,* Revised Standard Version, eds. Herbert G. May and Bruce M. Metzger (New York: Oxford University Press, 1973).

Printed in the United States
62606LVS00001B/1